W9-AGZ-451

✕   ✕   ✕

ALL ROADS
ARE GOOD

✕   ✕   ✕

ALL ROADS ARE GOOD

✖ ✖ ✖ ✖ ✖

NATIVE VOICES ON LIFE AND CULTURE

PUBLISHED BY THE SMITHSONIAN INSTITUTION PRESS
IN ASSOCIATION WITH THE NATIONAL MUSEUM OF THE
AMERICAN INDIAN, SMITHSONIAN INSTITUTION

Washington and London

© 1994 Smithsonian Institution. All rights reserved. No part of this book may be reproduced in any form without the prior permission of the Smithsonian Institution and the National Museum of the American Indian.

Published in conjunction with the exhibition *All Roads Are Good: Native Voices on Life and Culture*, on view at the National Museum of the American Indian, George Gustav Heye Center, Alexander Hamilton U.S. Custom House, New York City, 30 October 1994 – 1 February 1998.

Library of Congress Cataloging-in-Publication Data

All roads are good: native voices on life and culture / National Museum of the American Indian, Smithsonian Institution.
p. cm.
Published in conjunction with an exhibition held at the National Museum of the American Indian, New York City, Oct. 1994 – Feb. 1998.
Includes index.
ISBN 1-56098-451-1 (cloth : alk. paper). – ISBN 1-56098-452-X (paper : alk. paper)
1. Indians – Material culture – Exhibitions. 2. Indians – Social life and customs – Exhibitions. 3. National Museum of the American Indian (U.S.) – Exhibitions. I. National Museum of the American Indian (U.S.)
E56.A56 1994
970.004'97'0074753 – dc20   94-8236

British Library Cataloguing-in-Publication Data are available

Manufactured in the United States of America

01 00 99 98 97 96 95 94   5 4 3 2 1

⊗ The paper used in this publication meets the minimum requirements of the American National Standard for Permanence of Paper for Printed Library Materials Z39.48-1984.

For permission to reproduce illustrations appearing in this book, please correspond directly with the National Museum of the American Indian. The Smithsonian Institution Press does not retain reproduction rights for these illustrations individually.

All Roads Are Good is published with the assistance of a grant from the James Smithson Society.

Terence Winch: editor and project manager
Cheryl Wilson: assistant editor
Design by Grafik Communications, Ltd.
Typeset in Sabon and Matrix and printed on Consoweb Brilliant Dull.

Printed and bound by R. R. Donnelley & Sons. Cover and jacket printed by Phoenix Color.

The National Museum of the American Indian, Smithsonian Institution, is dedicated to working in collaboration with the indigenous peoples of the Americas to foster and protect native cultures throughout the Western Hemisphere. The museum's publishing program seeks to augment awareness of Native American beliefs and lifeways, and to educate the public about the history and significance of native cultures.

Cover: Sioux beaded deerskin (detail). See figure 44.

Title page: Moccasins and other footwear from the NMAI collection.

Page 7: Moccasin. Chippewa. 19.6341 (detail).

Page 8: Crazy Horse's shirt (detail). See figure 41.

Page 11: Pomo three-stick coiled basket (detail). See figure 89.

Page 13: Quechua *unkuña* (detail). See figure 76.

TABLE OF CONTENTS

I studied under
Grandpa Fools Crow,
a Lakota holy man. He said never
bad-mouth anybody,
never be envious or jealous
of anybody; if you are, you won't
be on the right road yourself,
'cause all roads are good.

ABE CONKLIN

For me, *All Roads Are Good: Native Voices on Life and Culture* represents the important first effort of the National Museum of the American Indian to do precisely what is suggested by the book's title — bring the essential voices of native peoples themselves to the interpretation of our cultures and the things we have made.

For much of our recent history, non-native scholars and others have been the principal interpreters of our lives and lifeways. I believe that many of these contributions to scholarship and cultural representation have been worthy and have added much to our collective knowledge of the complex and diverse historic and contemporary cultures of the Americas that are our shared heritage.

The contents of this book, however, mark the public beginning of the museum's determination to include in a systematic way our own voices in this body of cultural representation. In contemplating this proposition, I often reflect on the metaphor used by David Hurst Thomas, an archaeologist of the Americas and a member of the museum's board of trustees, in his insightful introductory essay to volume three of *Columbian Consequences*. There he explains that a "cubist" approach capable of looking at native culture from multiple viewpoints is essential to sound and creative scholarship. He also emphasizes that this approach is required by a fundamental fact of cultural interpretation: " . . . to one degree or another, all views of the human past are created by those telling the story."

What you will read in the pages that follow are the stories of twenty-three native people from throughout the Western Hemisphere who were invited to the museum to make selections from our collections and to tell you in their own unfiltered voices why this cultural patrimony is important to them and how it reflects and defines their cultural realities. The stories you hear will be as varied as the selectors who tell them — they are artists, teachers, elders, and community leaders. What joins them together is their deep knowledge of, and personal commitment to, native life and culture.

I will leave to your own sense of discovery the particular insights and information you take away from this book, but I offer for your consideration several themes that the selectors' comments evoke for me. Notwithstanding the powerful aesthetic qualities of much of indigenous creativity, the objects are also important for what they tell us about the thinking of the people who made them and the often fundamental distinctions between that thinking and Western European world views. In discussing her selection of a Mimbres pot, for example, Rina Swentzell, a Tewa-Santa Clara Pueblo artist and architect, explains the difference:

Po-wa-ha *("water-wind-breath") is the creative energy of the world, the breath that makes the wind blow and the water flow. Within Mimbres pots, several world levels are usually depicted, showing the human, animal, and plant realms. Around them are the mountains and surrounding everything is the breath that flows completely around. That's why they're so enormous and all-encompassing — because they suggest the breath that flows around the whole world.*

The comments of selectors also frequently offer poignant insights into the contemporary state of mind of native peoples toward indigenous arts and cultures. Earl Nyholm, a renowned Ojibwe artisan and linguist, worries openly that culture has become dangerously fractured:

Ojibwe culture today is like a raw egg that is dropped and scattered, so all that is left is pieces. The pieces represent certain hardcore people throughout Ojibwe country. If you could collect these carriers of tradition together in one area, then you could make the egg whole again.

Rina Swentzell expresses her similar concern about the potential destructive cultural impact of commercialism and commodification on native arts:

I think Native Americans are running after sophisticated art. They want to become studio artists, which takes them away from the real essence of native art. A lot of recent work involves highly contrived objects that are out of context – again, the opposite of the woman's way of doing things. The best native work is about remembering, and I think we're starting to forget.

Others face this understandable cultural anxiety with remarkable determination – as does Susan Billy, an accomplished Pomo basket-weaver:

. . . I get very upset when I hear people say that it is a dying art and that nobody is doing it, because I'm here, I'm doing it. And I know that there are others also weaving. I feel that there is always somebody who is going to carry on that wisdom and that knowledge.

Thus, in *All Roads Are Good: Native Voices on Life and Culture*, you will hear the many voices that are Native America. We will tell you about the past that has guided our lives and our cultures for the millennia, and we will express openly our anxieties concerning our cultural present – and, perhaps most important, we want you to hear from us our hopes and aspirations for our future.

✕

This book and the accompanying exhibition would not have been possible without the work of many dedicated people. We are, first of all, greatly indebted to the twenty-three selectors whose words, ideas, insights, and judgments made the entire project come to life. We also want to thank several initial participants in the project, who provided us with valuable help: George Horse Capture, John Kim Bell, Victor Masayesva, Juan Hernandez, and Jacinto Arias. We are especially grateful to selector Abe Conklin, who gave us the phrase "all roads are good," which perfectly summed up the spirit of this project.

We owe significant thanks to the James Smithson Society, which provided a generous grant that helped make the production of this book possible.

The text of the book was put together from thousands of pages of transcriptions and background material by the NMAI Publications Office. Terence Winch, Acting Head of Publications, edited the text, with help from assistant editor Cheryl Wilson. Editorial assistant Lou Stancari and secretary Ann Kawasaki helped with the many details involved in creating the final product. The museum's curatorial staff – Eulalie Bonar, Cécile Ganteaume, Mary Jane Lenz, and Nancy Rosoff – coordinated the selection process and conducted the original interviews with the selectors around which the project has revolved. They also reviewed the manuscript of this book and made many useful suggestions. Special assistant Rick Hill oversaw the development of the text and helped resolve issues involving content. Assistant Director Clara Sue Kidwell lent her keen scholarly eye to textual matters. Alyce Sadongei read the manuscript and offered helpful advice. Sharon Dean, Pamela Dewey, Karen Furth, Janine Jones, Danyelle Means, and Laura Nash of the NMAI Photography Archives were instrumental in keeping the photography required for the book and exhibition moving forward. Judy Kirpich and the staff of Grafik Communications are responsible for the imaginative "look" of this publication. Irene Coray provided valuable translation help. Photographer David Heald and mountmaker Elizabeth McKean worked long and hard to produce the stunning color illustrations of objects from the collection that you will see herein. Chief Conservator Marian Kaminitz, along with Scott Merritt and Leslie Williamson, helped prepare the objects for this publication and for the exhibition.

David Neel contributed many of the excellent photographic portraits of the selectors in the book and exhibition. Pablita Abeyta, NMAI Congressional Liaison, offered valuable advice, and Dan Agent of the Office of Public Affairs lent his expertise to our efforts at heightening public awareness of the museum. Finally, we are pleased to collaborate on this project with the staff of Smithsonian Institution Press, in particular Dan Goodwin, Amy Pastan, Hilary Reeves, and Ken Sabol, who worked diligently to meet a very demanding production schedule.

The exhibition was likewise the result of many devoted people who extended themselves to produce a complex show on a tight schedule. Nearly everyone on our staff played one role or another in this exhibition, but several should be singled out. Jim Volkert, Project Director, guided the project from inception to installation, gently coaxing both the project and the team to their best efforts. Karen Fort, Project Manager, orchestrated all the planning and details that put form to the ideas, including coordinating schedules and budget, scripting, design, fabrication, installation, and general project administration. Cécile Ganteaume, Assistant Curator, assisted in the development of the content presentation; Carolyn Rapkievian, Public Programs Coordinator, was the audience advocate; Peter Brill, Curator of Exhibits, coordinated countless tasks in New York; conservator Marian Kaminitz managed the review and conservation of each artifact on display and was instrumental in finding solutions to numerous exhibition challenges while ensuring the safety of the artifacts. Thanks are also due to George Arevalo, Margaret Dimond, Joe Cross, Andrea Gaines, Perry Ground, Sherry Huhndorf, Rachel Lax, and Randi Posner, who provided invaluable assistance throughout the selection process by helping to make the collections accessible to the selectors, documenting the artifact selections, and recording the selectors' comments. Olivia Cadaval, Veronica Cereceda, José Luis Krafft, Pilar Larreamendi de Moscoso, Rachel Nava-Mercado, Oswaldo Rivera Sundt, and Irene Zimmermann de la Torre served as translators and facilitators for the Latin American selectors. Catherine Benamou, José Montaño, Marty Kreipe de Montaño, Lydia Moñtes, Nancy Rosoff, and Erica C. Wortham also provided translating and other research assistance for the Latin American selectors. Marion Marino provided secretarial help and Fred Nahwooksy was responsible for planning and managing the research-gathering phase of the project. Lance Belanger helped facilitate the selectors' visits to New York City. Clinton Elliott of NMAI and Fred Barney Taylor of Maestro Video Productions coordinated the videotaping of the selectors.

In addition to the initial selectors, the following helped to further refine and focus the content: Harding Big Bow, leader in the Native American Church; Ted Coe, curator for *Lost and Found Traditions*; Dorothy Grant, fashion designer; G. Peter Jemison, director of the Ganondagan Historic Site; Nancy Mitchell, anthropologist; June Nash, anthropologist at the City University of New York; Margot Scheville, specialist in Central American textiles at the Phoebe Hearst Museum at the University of California, Berkeley; and Clifford Trafzer, historian, scholar, author, and director of the Ethnic Studies Department at University of California, Riverside.

Special acknowledgement must go to the design firm of Krent/Paffett Associates, Inc., and their project manager Barbara Stewart Smith, for their sensitivity to the requirements of the project, their successful organizational and design solutions, and their unfailing good humor throughout the evolution of this exhibit. The final realization of the exhibition is greatly indebted to the able fabrication and installation of Rathe Productions Incorporated, and to the media design and production firm of Monadnock Media, Inc. Although seldom mentioned in acknowledgments, this project could not have been completed without the able and often invisible support of the Smithsonian's Office of Design and Construction and Office of Contracts and Property Management.

W. Richard West, Jr., Director
(Southern Cheyenne and member of the Cheyenne and Arapaho Tribes of Oklahoma)

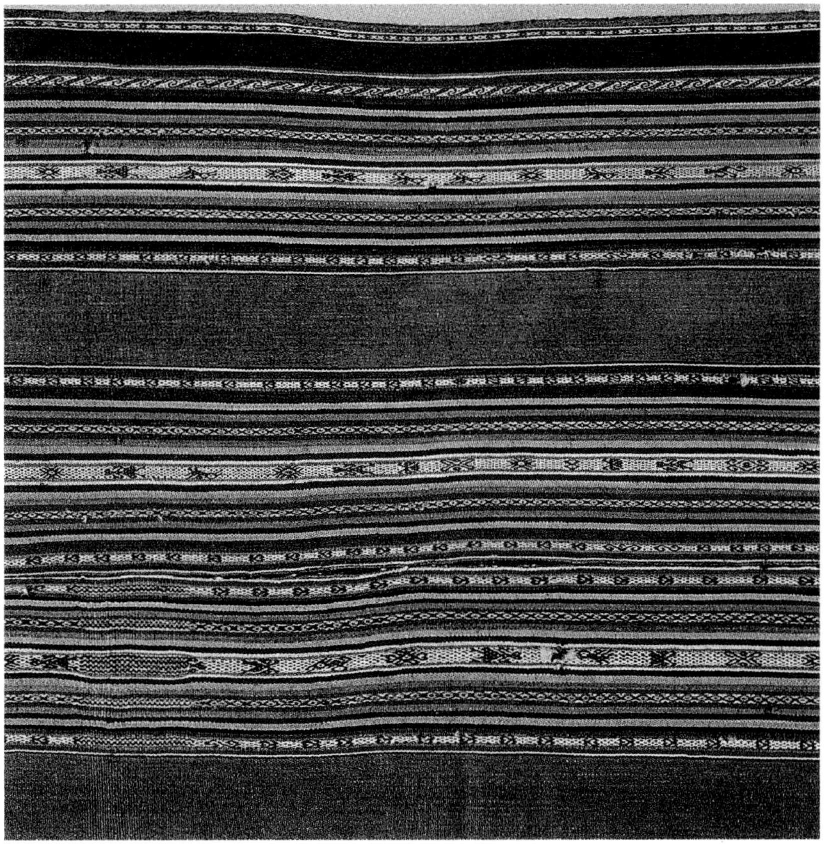

There is a rule about jingle dresses that my mother mentioned to me once. Jingle dresses are worn by women for dancing in the traditional Chippewa (Anishinabeg) way. They are festooned with rows of small, shiny metal cones that used to be, and occasionally still are, made from the lids of snuff tins. The skill of the dancer can be judged by the rhythm of the sound the dress produces. The rule my mother mentioned is that you don't mix jingles made from Copenhagen cans with those made from Skoal cans, because the tones of the two don't harmonize.

The rule underscores the most important dimension of a jingle dress — it is made to be heard as well as seen, and to be heard, it must move. The rhythmic clink, the metallic flash in the sun, are part of the dress as surely as the materials of which it is made. Metal snuff cans came in with white traders and settlers, so it is obvious that jingle dresses post-date European contact for the Chippewa around Lake Superior. The jingle dress today, however, is very much the sign of a woman who knows and values her cultural roots and has learned the distinctive way of dancing that makes the dress she wears a thing of sound and beauty.

My great-aunt donated her jingle dress, along with other items, to a county historical museum in Minnesota, where it probably languishes in a box on a shelf. Even displayed, it would be a static thing, silent and motionless. Chippewa women, viewing that object on display, can enliven it in their minds through their memories of powwows and of family traditions that delineated how dresses were made, and by whom, and for what purpose. The non-Indian, or even non-Chippewa, viewer may see the colorful material, the shiny cones, and the painstaking hand-stitching, but could easily miss the real significance that the dress has.

These different ways of viewing things confer different kinds of validity. A museum endows an object with importance because it represents some kind of cultural value. The object may represent a certain style of craft work, or it may be unique, or it may meet certain aesthetic standards. Museums become arbiters of meaning in the very process of establishing collecting plans and acquiring objects.

Indian people who have lived with objects, on the other hand, bring a different perspective to museum collections. The basket may evoke memories of watching a basketmaker at work. A fringed buckskin dress recalls the hypnotic swaying of many fringed garments as dancers move around a circle to the insistent beating of a drum. The blanket draped over a mannequin recalls the weaver at her loom, the bleating of the sheep, the pungent smell of dyestuffs simmering in a pot.

The National Museum of the American Indian, established as part of the Smithsonian Institution in 1989, is young, as museums go, although its collections date back to the early part of the twentieth century. The museum's commitment to reflecting native perspectives is apparent in the exhibition called *All Roads Are Good: Native Voices on Life and Culture* and in this complementary book. To initiate the museum's first major exhibition at its new facility — the George Gustav Heye Center at the Alexander Hamilton U.S. Custom House in New York City — W. Richard West, Jr., the museum's director, invited twenty-three native people from throughout the Americas to select objects from NMAI's vast collections and to talk about the reasons for their selections. The native voices and perspectives recounted in this book also inform the exhibition. Richard W. Hill, Sr., Special

Assistant to the Director and a member of the Tuscarora nation in upstate New York, was invited to be curator of the show to guide its overall development.

Both book and exhibition have grown out of an organic process of interaction. Members of the museum's curatorial staff – Mary Jane Lenz, Eulalie Bonar, Nancy Rosoff, and Cécile Ganteaume – worked with the selectors, showing them the riches of the collection and discussing objects with them. Transcriptions of the videotaped discussions were used as the basis for the text of the book, which, like the exhibition, was the result of a process in which the selectors worked with the museum's publications staff – including Terence Winch and Cheryl Wilson – to create the final product.

The "roads" of the title represent the varying cultural backgrounds and ways of viewing objects that the selectors brought to the process of choosing. The reasons for their choices do not necessarily reflect the standards of aesthetic or historic value that might inform displays in an anthropology or history museum. Rather, objects become expressions of distinct ways of seeing the world, an entree for the viewer into a different cultural understanding of the collection. Some common themes emerged during the selection process – the nature of the sacred, relationships with the environment, responsibility to community, for example – but each individual expressed them in a unique way.

Not all of these visitors to the museum selected objects that represented their own cultural background. As with the snuff cans, forces beyond those of traditional Indian ways sometimes enter their lives. Some selectors are scholars who have studied the arts of many cultures – thus Lloyd Kiva New, a Cherokee from North Carolina, can be moved by the beauty and craftsmanship of Northwest Coast Sitka spruce-root hats. What appeals to him, however, is not the hat as object of craft, but the thought of a number of such hats worn by proud men walking through a village. The hat opens vistas of action.

George Gustav Heye, founder of the Museum of the American Indian in New York, whose collections form the basis of the National Museum of the American Indian, was evidently pas-

sionate in his pursuit of objects for their own sake, and perhaps for their very objectivity. A colleague described how he would descend on a community and buy up great quantities of things, even down to the dishrags. In his acquisitiveness, however, he preserved a collection of unparalleled richness that can illuminate many aspects of native life in the Americas.

The native people who selected the objects upon which this book and its accompanying exhibition are based now speak about them in ways quite different from anything Heye himself might have imagined. Would Heye have understood that what the selectors say about the objects is as important as the simple fact of their existence? I suspect not.

The photographic reproductions of the objects in this book are once removed from their physical reality in the world. Textures are not as readily apparent; one cannot walk around photographs to see all sides; there can only be the illusion of motion. The words in the book, however, give life to the objects because they are the words in which the selectors describe their actions, thoughts, and feelings. Through the power of the spoken word captured on the page, the selectors can add to the context of the object by evoking a sense of the immediacy of experience. In so doing, they create a more permanent record of what an object means to them.

In *All Roads Are Good*, the words of the selectors take their place beside the images of the objects to create a new way of looking at things. This book is intended to stand both with the exhibition (although there are objects illustrated in the book that are not in the exhibition, and vice versa) and independently, as a tribute to the power of native voices. The words evoke the mental images of when and how things were used and what they mean to people in their own cultural contexts. The essays in this book create the world of movement, action, and memory that gives the objects their special meaning. This book is an attempt to share the insights of people within indigenous cultures with those outside.

Clara Sue Kidwell, Assistant Director for Cultural Resources
(*Chippewa*)

· 15 ·

Joseph Medicine Crow, a highly regarded storyteller and respected elder of the Crow people, has established a reputation as one of the most authentic and authoritative voices in contemporary Native American life. Because of his extensive knowledge of Crow traditions, which includes first-hand familiarity with pre-reservation Crows, Medicine Crow is considered the historian of his people. He is the author of *From the Heart of Crow Country: The Crow Indians' Own Stories.*

His life has been marked by accomplishment — grandson of a scout who rode with Custer, he is the first member of his tribe to graduate from college, going on to earn a master's degree in anthropology. A World War II combat veteran, he is a teacher, writer, and lecturer who travels extensively. Medicine Crow lives in his native Montana.

"I talked to an old man here, some twenty years ago.... I asked him one time about thunderbirds. 'Did you ever see one?' He said, 'yes.' 'Tell me about thunderbirds,' I said. 'All right,' he said, 'I'll tell you.'"

· 17 ·

JOSEPH MEDICINE CROW

FIGURE 1
CROW SHIELD.
PAINTED BUCKSKIN WITH WEASEL SKIN
AND FEATHERS, 54 CM. (12.732)

BAXBE

The word *baxbe* can be interpreted in several ways, but basically it means the power — mysterious power, sacred power, what the white man likes to call medicine.

This power comes from the Supreme Power — God, who the Crows call the First Maker or the Creator. Baxbe comes from that ultimate source of power and is given to a person by the Supreme Being through an animal emissary, like an owl, eagle, or butterfly. Sometimes the emissaries are bears, wolves, and other animals.

You get the power by going on a vision questing experience or by fasting. And there you supplicate or make a blood offering by cutting the tips off your fingers, and so forth.

You suffer, you deny yourself all the natural comforts, like water, food, clothing. You do this so that the Supreme Power or the Great Spirit, as the white man likes to call it, will have mercy on you, pity on you, compassion on you, and give you so much of his power, so you can become invulnerable, turn away bullets, turn away ills, or somehow regulate and control the natural elements, like bad storms — a hailstorm or a tornado. So that's what baxbe is.

CURLY, CROW SCOUT
FOR LT. GEORGE CUSTER.
(P6647)

And if it's not symbolized on a shield, part of it is inside of what we call a medicine bundle. It's wrapped up in there and kept inside. The whole thing becomes sacred. And only the owner can open it at certain times.

So the baxbe can be represented on the shield or in a medicine bundle or even on a rock.

AKBADEAH

Akbadeah means he who uses baxbe, the power. That's what the white man calls a medicine man: akbadeah. The person with the power can do miracles. He can cure wounded persons, mend broken bones. He can cause severe weather — storms — to come. He can do wonders.

There are different kinds of medicine men. Some specialize in caring for wounds — battlefield wounds or wounds from animals. Some specialize in snakebite, skin disease, and all that. They're specialized at their work. And they all use the power, baxbe.

They use the power, so they are called user or doer or performer. Akbadeah means performer, one who makes things happen or prevents them from happening. There is also a visionary type of akbadeah who can forecast what's coming ahead. These visionaries prophesy, they don't doctor.

· 19 ·

Once in a while a man noted for possessing and using a certain gift of power would bestow some of that power on another person, or sell it. Sell the right. He would have to be approached and given presents and courted for some time before he'd bestow power.

This bestowal of power doesn't happen so often with shields. A shield is more of a personal insignia or stamp — kind of like the old European standards. So, they don't duplicate it often, if at all. Maybe once in a great while they will. A shield possesses individual symbolism, and whenever the camp was on the move, a wife would proudly display that symbol on the side of her saddle. But the akbadeah will make duplicate medicine rocks — maybe not as big, but some duplication of it. And then a young warrior would take that on a warpath.

SELECTION

The central figure in this shield is a thunderbird (fig. 2). The Crow Indians use the thunderbird quite a bit, because they regard the thunderbird as the most powerful baxbe. The Crows believe that the thunderbird has only two claws and they would depict the thunderbird to show that every time it opens its eyes, lightning would shoot out.

The butterfly depicted here was probably the personal medicine of the man who made the shield. That was his medicine. So every time he was ready to go on the warpath, or about to take part in some ceremonial occasion, he'd have a butterfly painted right on his chest or sometimes on his back. And of course, eagle feathers are always on shields — most are eagle feathers.

Whoever made this chose those symbols to represent a vision that he had while doing the fasting or the vision questing. Each shield is a personal symbolism devised by the man who had the dream, or saw it in a dream. Sometimes the symbolism is based on things that he actually saw or on an actual vision.

It's difficult to interpret these things. A shield like this means something to the person who made it. But none of us can know exactly what it means unless its maker tells us. And usually they don't want to tell it in detail — they'll just kind of give a rough idea. Maybe he can use this shield for rainmaking or preventing a serious storm from coming — it can go this way or that way. Or on the warpath it could be that this particular design would protect him and so forth. A shield like this has the power to confer invulnerability on its owner.

SUA'DAGAGAY / THUNDERBIRD

Sua'dagagay — *sua* means thunder, *dagagay* means bird. Like the Crows, the Blackfeet also have quite a bit of lore on the thunderbird concept. I don't know about the other tribes.

I talked to an old man some twenty years ago. He died in 1972, about two or three years after my grandmother died in 1969. He was an old storyteller by the name of Plain Feather. He died at 102. He was a real good storyteller.

I asked him one time about thunderbirds. "Did you ever see one?" He said, "yes." "Tell me about thunderbirds," I said. "All right," he said, "I'll tell you."

He mentioned a man who was riding horseback into the Pryor Mountains to look for his horses. And he got into a box canyon, known now as Lost Creek Canyon. As he was getting into this box canyon, he heard a noise, a swishing noise, and

FIGURE 2
CROW SHIELD.
PAINTED BUFFALO HIDE WITH FEATHERS,
56.5 CM. (12.7779)

looked out around and saw a big black bird coming toward the canyon. So he just quickly took cover under the cliffs there, and the big bird went right by him, right up the canyon. He said it was huge. Real huge black bird.

A couple of days later, word had come that south of there, in a little town called Bridger, Montana, a white man had killed a thunderbird. So, he said, a bunch of them took off to see it.

It was just about a half a day's ride from Pryor, Montana. "When we got there," he said, "people were still looking at the thunderbird. We measured its wing span from the tip of the wings — three men had to stand there to do it. It's huge."

He said he noticed that there were only two toes, about as big as a yearling calf's horn. It had black feathers. So he thought he saw one, but I think he saw a condor. And the last condor in Montana was killed in the early 1870s, around there. I don't know why they killed them off. White mountain men, trappers, killed them off. Why they did that, I don't know. They weren't bothering anybody.

There are all kinds of stories about people having encounters with thunderbirds, but I still think they're talking about condors. Tell you another story. There was a man by the name of Little Nest — my grandfather Medicine Crow's half-brother, so I called him grandfather. Little Nest related that when he was a young man, a boy, they were camped up there around Red Lodge someplace. There was a lake up in the mountains. And there's an island not too far from the shore with a few trees on it. And they could see a nest on the rock, and some birds — two of them, their heads sticking out. So he swam out there and got these two birds. Young birds, you know, still fuzzy.

So he got those two birds by the legs and swam out there with one arm. He brought these birds back to the camp, which wasn't too far from the lake. He put them on the ground there and people came to look at them.

All of a sudden a small cloud formed over the camp, and hail turned loose; lightning was striking everywhere. People just took cover, and some of the elders came and said, "Get rid of those birds. They're sacred birds. They're thunderbird chicks. Take them back quickly, right now, before some of us are killed."

So he grabbed the two birds again and swam back through that storm and put them back in their nest. And the storm quit all of a sudden.

When he first brought them and put the little birds on the ground, they were blind, he said. No eyes yet. Eyes closed. He would put the birds several yards apart and they would find each other without opening their eyes, they'd run to each other and wiggle together. They didn't open their eyes, so he didn't know lightning was going to attack. So there's another experience with thunderbirds.

Then, of course, we have legends about thunderbirds having confrontations with human beings. A man by the name of Brave Wolf was out hunting in the hills. And one evening he disappeared. He came back maybe a week or two later and related that while he was hunting, a great big thunderbird came and snatched him — took him to a high cliff, overlooking a lake up in the mountains.

And there on this rock was a nest with two chicks in it, just beginning to get big. The mother thunderbird said to him, "I have brought you up here for a purpose. In the spring when my

FIGURE 3
CROW CHILD'S SHIRT.
HIDE, WITH BEADS AND WOOL,
LENGTH 42 CM. (13.7133)

young ones are just about so big, a monster would come out of that water down there and climb up this cliff. It will devour my little ones. It's been doing that for quite a while. And I've tried everything to stop that monster. I hit it with my lightning and I couldn't stop it. So now I have brought you, a human being, to come and help me." "All right," he said, "let me think about it, see what I can do." Then he said, "Go out and get me some logs. Dry logs. I want to build a fire. We'll pile it up here." So the thunderbird took off and pretty soon came back with a dried log and limbs and piled it up pretty high. "Now," he said, "I'll need some nice round rocks." So the thunderbird went off and brought some rocks in, and soon he had a nice pile of rocks. "All right," he said, "I'll need water. Just about the time that this monster is going to move, let me know a day ahead of time. I'll need water then."

After a while, the mother

CHIEF MEDICINE CROW (RIGHT),
LEADING A DANCE.
CHARLES RAU COLLECTION. (P9343)

thunderbird started noticing the signs — water started picking up waves and so forth. She said to him, "It's coming up in about a day." "All right," he says, "I need water."

But before that time, the man had ordered the thunderbird to kill a large buffalo, which she did and brought it up to him. He skinned it, took the hide, and made kind of a basket with willows around it so it would hold water. Then the thunderbird caused a little quick shower and filled that container full of water.

So the water was right there. Then he started building a fire and heating the rocks right near the edge, where the monster would come up.

Then the thing started coming up — the waves started moving up pretty high. It was a great big snake — a dragon, I suppose. And when it started coming up, the mother thunderbird would go down and strike it with lightning. But

FIGURE 4
CROW HEADDRESS.
OWL AND EAGLE FEATHERS, WOOL TRADE CLOTH,
AND BUFFALO HIDE, 142 X 33 CM. (15.2393)

she couldn't stop it — it kept coming up slowly, slowly, slowly, getting pretty close to the top. By that time, it opened its mouth.

So the man made a couple of forks out of limbs so he could push the burning rock into that dragon's mouth. He kept throwing red-hot rocks into its mouth. And when all the rocks were down the monster's throat, he poured water down there. And the steam shot up and made all kinds of hissing noises and the old dragon started wobbling around, groaning, and finally it fell backwards into the lake with a big splash.

And the thunderbird invited all the birds of the country to come and have a big feast. So the birds came and ate this monster. They ate it up, eventually. In the meantime, she brought the man back.

And the Crow Indians believe that lake is the one called Jenny Lake in Jackson, up near Jackson, Wyoming, in the Grand Tetons.

CLAN SYSTEMS AND CROW HISTORY

We still use our clan system quite a bit. In our games and tournaments, certain clans compete against each other. We know the clans quite well. One knows his or her patrilineal clan and matrilineal clan. In school, in some of our Headstart classes, we try to teach the young ones the clan laws and the clan system. They're pretty well versed on it, so they keep it up. I think that's what makes the Crows Indians, so to speak. The tribes that have lost their clan system don't have much of a cultural base.

The so-called River Crows (a band of the Crow tribe) once lived above the Missouri River in what is now the state of Montana. When the Crows moved to this part of the reservation, the River Crows stayed north of present-day Harden, Montana, along the Big Horn

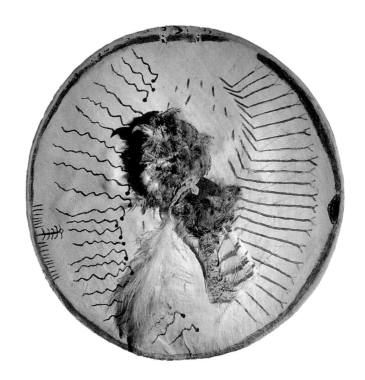

FIGURE 5
CROW SHIELD.
PAINTED BUFFALO HIDE WITH OWL ORNAMENT,
54 CM. (11.7681)

River. And the Mountain Crows (the other band of the Crow tribe) are more or less higher up Big Horn River and Little Big Horn River.

Kicked in the Bellies is a clan originally known as Whistling Waters. This Whistling Waters Clan would prefer to live up by the headwaters of Wind River, in what is now the state of Wyoming. Years ago, the Whistling Waters Clan seceded from the Mountain Crows and moved over into Wyoming, around the headwaters of Wind River, and stayed there.

They quit going on the warpath because they were far removed from the Cheyenne, the Hairy Nostrils (Gros Ventre), the Assiniboine, and other tribes. And there, in the Wind River country, it was fairly quiet. They raised good horses and lived well — rich, kind of. And they were then called Whistling Waters. Then an incident happened a long time ago that earned them the name Kicked in the Bellies. A war party had ventured south toward Utah, up the Green River, which Crows used to call Fat River, in wild western Wyoming. They brought back a stallion, their first horse, and took him to their camp near present-day Lander, Wyoming. And they were milling around that animal, looking at it — there ain't no such animal, they thought. It looked like an elk, it's got round hooves, a bushy tail, and ears like an elk. One of them got a little bit too close to the horse's tail and the horse kicked him right in the belly with both hind legs. He kicked him over. And everyone had a big laugh out of that and called him One Who's Kicked in the Belly. After a while, the whole clan was called Kicked in the Bellies. That was a nickname.

SPIRITUALITY AND STRONG MEDICINE

Religion is more or less individualized by the Crows, except for the Sun Dance, which involves the whole tribe. With most of the shields, as I mentioned before, there's a spiritual experience, philosophical significance, involved — these symbols represent something that only the shield's maker knows but others don't. Unless he tells it to somebody, it remains a mystery.

A shield may depict bullets, which may mean that the owner has a medicine that repels enemy bullets, making him invulnerable. And in a time of battle, when he is surrounded, he can grunt like a buffalo and the bullets won't hurt him at all. I've heard stories that when warriors are surrounded by the enemy, they'll grunt like a buffalo or a bear, or whatever, imitating their animal protectors. This gives them extra strength, bravery, and invulnerability. A man may have more than one animal protector.

Bull Goes Hunting, Little Nest's father and my great-grandfather, was quite a medicine man. And he made strong medicine for my grandfather, Medicine Crow. His younger son, Little Nest, was a little bit too late for the intertribal war days, but his medicine was horses. So the medicine that Bull Goes Hunting made for his younger son is represented by the acquisition of horses. Little Nest was a great horseman. But Medicine Crow's own medicine, plus the one originally made for him by Bull Goes Hunting, resulted in his becoming a chief by the age of twenty-two. He did all kinds of war deeds. I know twenty-two of them. There is a word for that — *alaxchiia*. It means deeds, war deeds, coups.

Rina Swentzell (Tewa-Santa Clara Pueblo) received her M.A. in architecture and Ph.D. in American studies from the University of New Mexico. A consultant to architectural firms and nonprofit institutions such as museums and schools, Swentzell also writes and lectures on the philosophical basis of the Pueblo world and its educational, artistic, and architectural expressions. An advisor for program planning at NMAI, she was also a contributor to the museum's first major publication *Native American Dance: Ceremonies and Social Traditions* (1992).

Swentzell's aesthetic approach to Native American art embraces work from throughout the Western Hemisphere. Of particular concern to her is the increasing commercialization of Native American art and the negative effect of this materialistic shift on contemporary native artists.

"Artists today are so self-conscious — they go into their studios with these big plans in their heads about what they're going to do and how they're going to do it and it's all very rational, very self-conscious. Art today is a very deliberate act. I feel, however, that art comes from a deeper source somewhere — it's part of the act of just living: you know, let's put on the beans and get the clay out."

RINA SWENTZELL

· 29 ·

HOPI WOMAN WITH JAR.

ARIZONA. (P18709)

AESTHETICS AND SPIRITUAL POWER

I think that traditional Native American art is characterized by a very strong sense of design, a strong sense of form. There is a powerful aesthetic sense that can be seen, touched, and felt in the created objects.

There is a strong connection in the work of different native groups. I find myself responding with such intensity, awe, and wonder. I feel a very strong need to express that connection among these groups. I want to be able to say, "Hey, look at all of us — look at what we can do, at what we've done." The aesthetic sense is so well honored in traditional societies. So many of these works are so beautiful. It's just incredible. It's remarkable that people, in the ordinary course of their lives, come out with these exquisite things. If you do it with any care at all, it comes out exquisite — that's a human trait.

Modern Indian people can derive strength from the objects that their ancestors have made because of the incredible power and energy that these things have — not only in terms of cultural and spiritual meaning, but in aesthetic quality as well. There is strength in the aesthetic beauty of these objects.

The spiritual strength and energy of these objects go with me wherever I go. I feel that I can draw from them whenever I need to. I would like to see some of the power in these objects go back into the communities. I'm *not* talking about the objects them-selves going back. I'm talking about the strength of what's contained in them getting back into the communities in some form or another. That flow of energy has to go back again into native communities.

Native American art comes from a deeper place within the soul than any impulse growing out of commercial motives. Yet today we are seeing highly polished, non-utilitarian work coming out of Santa Clara and all the Pueblos. Some of this work seems to have no sense of the process involved — instead there is this overglaze of commercialism that is very disturbing to me.

I'm not asking that people go back and make things out of some anachronistic homage to the past. I just want us to be aware of the changes that are taking place. There is a cultural shift, an aesthetic change, occurring. By aesthetics I mean the proportion, the colors, the way something is made — those elements are shifting subtly and blatantly. I've seen these changes, for example, in the work of many contemporary weavers. I don't believe these shifts happen at the conscious level. But I'm convinced they are happening — I can see the shift in people's work, I can feel it in my hands, I can see it with my eyes, I can sense it.

There's been a change in our souls, in our being, that we're not acknowledging. But it comes through, it shows in everything we touch, everything we do.

FEMALE/MALE

In traditional societies, it is acknowledged that women do things in a different way than men. They take care of their kids, feed people, make clothes, without announcing it to the world. They conduct themselves in a much gentler, quieter way. The works I'm drawn to reflect this feminine element — they're about women doing what they need to be doing, but doing it carefully and in the best way they can. And when I sit around with other women making pots, I can just feel this female spirit coming out of their arms. Those pots just come out of our arms and out of our souls in a way that is quiet and doesn't call for attention.

Those great big generous pots express something quite the opposite of the ritual things created by men, which often exclude people — you know, the attitude that "this is important stuff. Don't come near it." With women, that kind of attitude is hardly ever an issue. Women have a wonderful openness and inclusiveness.

There are men who are very female and women who are very male. What I'm suggesting is that feminine energies are distinctly different from masculine energies and activities. But either of these energies can be embraced and expressed by any individual, male or female.

Spontaneity is a part of it — the more you get into planning something, the more you are following a male impulse. Some of the Mayan pottery I've looked at — work that clearly took some real concentration — could not have been made while stirring the stew and taking care of a couple of kids. That kind of sophistica-

tion, that focused, structured way of doing something, may be exactly what most people look for in a work of art. It's an approach that implies a particular way of ordering your world and your society. I think that the Maya and other Central American societies really did start going in that direction. What we have in the Southwest, on the other hand, was much more spontaneous. That's what I find so exciting about Pueblo work — its gentleness, spontaneity, a spirit of non-selfconsciousness, non-deliberateness. Women generally are more that way — more spontaneous because they're capable of doing multiple things at once. A man gets so focused. I can give myself over to my male side and become very focused, specific, and detailed.

I'm not suggesting that women are sloppy about what they do — the objects I selected make that clear. They just follow a different way. I think work done by women is much more incorporative of many things at once.

Some of the more spontaneous pots reveal organic levels that flow into each other. With one big Santa Clara pot, for instance, there are finger marks, polish marks, slip marks — but one thing flows into the other to finally come out with an exquisite form.

I think Native Americans are running after sophisticated art. They want to become studio artists, which takes them away from the real essence of native art. A lot of recent work involves highly contrived objects that are out of context — again, the opposite of the woman's way of doing things. The best native work is about remembering, and I think we're starting to forget.

YOUNG HAWASUPAI WOMAN MAKING BASKET.
ARIZONA. (P7934)

POTTERY

Pottery is an especially feminine activity. There is a conspicuous element of play involved in making pots and it really comes through when you watch, or when you are part of, the whole process: My mother, my aunt, my sisters, everybody's sitting around the table making a pot, everybody's making their pot. Children come in, grab a piece of clay and start to play with it. Meantime, everyone is talking and laughing and saying "why'd you do that?" and the adults are playing with the clay as much as the kids are. It's not this great big serious thing. People are cooking their beans while they're taking care of their kids and talking to neighbors. The whole experience seems to flow out of an unconscious place.

Artists today are so self-conscious — they go into their studios with these big plans in their heads about what they're going to do and how they're going to do it and it's all very rational, very self-conscious. Art today is a very deliberate act. I feel, however, that art comes from a deeper source some-where — it's part of the act of just living: you know, let's put on the beans and get the clay out. Pottery has always involved a social gathering. When you're

FIGURE 6
MIMBRES VALLEY BOWL.
NEW MEXICO. PAINTED CLAY,
DIAM. 27 CM. (4.3461)

sitting there making something with your family day after day, everybody gets good at it. Still, it's not the real focus of activity. It is one thing that you do in your day, in the course of every-day life. And out of that activity comes something from a deeper place in your being. But that's changing now because money has gotten involved and pots are becoming more precious — if a pot breaks, you've just lost six hundred dollars and that becomes very significant.

SELECTIONS

Po-wa-ha ("water-wind-breath") is the creative energy of the world, the breath that makes the wind blow and the water flow. Within Mimbres pots, several world levels are usually depicted, showing the human, animal, and plant realms. Around them are the mountains and surrounding everything is the breath that flows completely around. That's why they're so enormous and all-encompassing — because they suggest the breath that flows around the whole world. Two Mimbres bowls wonderfully depict po-wa-ha (figs. 6, 7).

The patterns of these two bowls, both very characteristic of Mimbres pottery, are based on Southwest mythology. There is the center world, where people, plants, and animals live, surrounded by the mountains. The wonderful, billowing cloud forms swirl with the wind around the mountains. You can see the play between light and dark areas, positive and negative spaces, and sense the breath that gives everything its energy. The way light and dark play off each other is a typical feature of these works. In the cloud bowl, the primary pattern could be either the dark or the white, depending on how you look at it. They are constantly playing with illusion. It's a wonderful technique.

Mimbres work also seems to play with the different boundaries of life. The world is distinctly organized into different levels — there are concentric rings around which everything happens, one ring within another. If you look at any Mimbres pot, it pretty much works that way. It's the idea of context, everything within a context. Both of these bowls are excellent examples of this aesthetic.

One of the bowls pictures a bear with a man superimposed over it, both of them sharing a diamond-shaped form. The way the bear and the man overlap — with one form going into the other — is once again very

typical. They both share the quadrilateral figures inside the diamond form, which, with its four-part movement, suggests the zoning of the world as well as the ways in which we are divided up within ourselves. I also see the diamond form as suggesting the rhythmic motion of the heart that both the man and the bear share. The intertwining of the human and animal is a central theme in Mimbres pottery.

The other bowl is very different — the "center world" is empty and the piece focuses on mountains and clouds. It doesn't depict the human-animal connection, but instead emphasizes the environment — the swirling clouds and wind. The forms here could possibly be waves as well, suggesting po-wa-ha, in which the three forces — water-wind-breath — are brought together.

Opposites are necessary in the Pueblo world view — they are there whether you see them or not. The Mimbres pots give a clear sense of this world view. Everything is dark and white, everything has two sides to it. Pueblo people are always playing with the notion of male and female, opposites that are contained in all of us; we're both dark and light at the same time.

FIGURE 7
MIMBRES BOWL.
NEW MEXICO. PAINTED CLAY,
DIAM. 27 CM. (24.6890)

· 35 ·

That oppositional tension just flows through the world.

✖

The *sikyatki* pot has a wonderful billowing fullness and a strong sense of center (fig. 8). The shape is typical of the work of Nampeyo. As a potter, I know how difficult it is to get that shape – the Hopis, particularly Nampeyo, were skilled at this. The painted design has all the elements of a sikyatki design, including a bird, the four directions, and four mountains. The design expresses the Pueblo notion of centering because the point at which the four mountains intersect is the physical center of the universe. The center point symbolically represents the place where the Pueblo people came from – the underworld – and it remains the center of their physical world. Southwest designs always relate human relationships to the cosmos.

✖

I've always been familiar with the design of this basket (fig. 9). It's made by the Tohono O'Odham and Akimel O'Odham tribes of Arizona. They have their own stories about the meaning of the design. Some people refer to it as a maze basket, but Indian people always tell me that it is not a maze because there's no exit. The human figure looks like he might be walking into a maze, but in reality everything leads to the center.

✖

Dough bowls, used for making large quantities of yeast bread, were brought into New Mexico after the Spanish introduced grain into the region. They came into existence just at the time when Indians began to feed enormous numbers of people during the feast days, which had become very popular. Non-Indians started coming into the Pueblos expecting to be fed. It still goes on today. You can walk into any of the Pueblos during feast days and you'll get fed – and, of course, nobody pays. Our family will feed four to five hundred people in one day. It is part of the whole idea of who we are as a people – we're supposed to embrace people, take them in and give them something to eat. When you go to Santo Domingo, the people will take you by the hand and say, "come eat with us." That is how this very generous bowl that just opens up, suggesting the act of feeding people, evolved. The dough bowl represents bountifulness. Once again, very female qualities – nurturing, giving, feeding, cooking – are at work.

This bowl captures another side of the Santo Domingo people (fig. 10). It's almost as if the leaves depicted on the outside are dancing around the rim. It's very exciting. The three buckskin thongs that somebody used to repair the bowl actually add to the feeling of lightness. For me, the design makes the whole pot just lift up. That's what I love about this bowl – it's got incredible movement. Unlike some dough bowls that just sit there, this one lifts up and wants to dance. For me, it's a wonderfully uplifting, joyous pot.

FIGURE 8
SIKYATKI-STYLE POT.
MADE BY NAMPEYO, HOPI-TEWA. PAINTED ARIZONA CLAY,
33.6 X 17.2 CM. (18.7533)

FIGURE 9
PIMA BASKET TRAY.
ARIZONA. VEGETAL FIBERS, DIAM.
24.8 CM. (11.415)

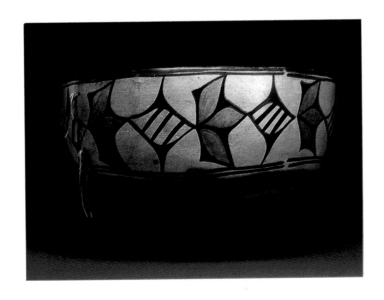

FIGURE 10
SANTO DOMINGO PUEBLO DOUGH BOWL, CA. 1910.
NEW MEXICO. PAINTED POLYCHROME REPAIRED WITH BUCKSKIN THONGS,
49 X 28.3 CM. (23.2472)

Lloyd Kiva New (Cherokee) is former director of the Institute of American Indian Arts in Santa Fe. A respected voice in Native American culture, New is a designer, entrepreneur, and arts educator. Enriched by his background as an arts professional, his perspective on Native American art and culture is at once sophisticated and straightforward.

For New, an exhibition has to have something of a theatrical element to succeed in delivering its message to a contemporary audience. He feels that the criterion used to present any Indian object should be its sublime, aesthetic expressiveness. For him, it is crucial that an overload of information not distance people from their visual experience of a compelling work of art.

· 39 ·

"People and cultures — like any living organisms — have to adapt to environmental changes; those that don't, die. The relationship of the past to the future has been stated in many ways — I like the declaration that 'the future lies in the future, not in the past.'"

LLOYD KIVA NEW

INDIANS, ART, AND THE FUTURE

Indians have lived on this continent for thousands of years. They developed spiritually oriented belief systems and practical ways of living with the forces of nature that served them very well until the sixteenth century, at which time these belief systems came into severe conflict with those of the Indians' scientifically driven Western conquerors. While the situation is gradually abating, it has not yet been completely resolved; many Indians are still very reluctant to exchange their ways for those of a scientifically and materialistically oriented dominant society. This battle of contrasting values goes on, creating a cultural no-man's-land in which many Indians suffer varying levels of cultural anomie, and commensurate social and economic dysfunction.

This essay is the result of an invitation from the National Museum of the American Indian to survey the museum's collection with an eye toward determining its best use in service to the Indian community. A small group, representing a range of tribal and professional backgrounds and points of view, was invited to select works from the museum's collection that caught our fancy — for whatever reasons — and to comment on them. I shall attempt to show a relationship between the museum, its collection, and the future of Indians.

While studying the collections of NMAI, I was struck by the vast number and range of items in the collection and by the proportion of high quality artworks it contains. From there I moved to a concern that there seemed to be a very wide range of variation and some serious black holes in the overall collection pattern — some tribes are represented by a multitude of pieces, some by very few, and many are not represented at all. I soon began to view the collection as a metaphorical handprint of the overall decline and corresponding breakdowns in cultural solidarity and economic independence in Native American history.

Notwithstanding these thoughts, my personal reaction was one of elation — of immense pride in seeing so many examples of high cultural accomplishment — and a corresponding flush of hope that what happened once can be made to happen again; if not a revival or duplication, perhaps a new expression of high cultural accomplishment would be possible. I must confess that I did not feel as much hope for the revival of "the good old days" as I did for the possible reconstruction of culturally disheveled tribal structures and an accompanying revival of the kind of can-do spirit that carried all tribal groups to varying levels of success in the past.

Since history so rarely repeats itself, I felt that I should base my case on the importance of finding good substitutes for what we have lost. For example, I didn't think that there was any chance of ever replacing the flamboyant buffalo period, and consequently, it might be time to slowly let go of such attachments to the past in favor of some other kind of self-directed cultural development.

At the same time, I felt that traditional belief systems might be ritualized and used as a spiritual bulwark for people desperately in need of some kind of valid cultural continuity. Although I did not hope for the duplication of the old ways, of course, or even for the revival of certain traditional art forms, I couldn't help but hope there might be a way to capture the meaning and poetry of better times through an active development in the arts that would give heart to future generations.

HAIDA HOUSE POSTS, 1882.

MASSET, BRITISH COLUMBIA. PHOTO BY R. MAYNARD. (P8922)

This was not a new thought; I had seen the process work very effectively with young people coming to the Institute of American Indian Arts back in the 1960s. Many students of the period declared their experiences at the institute to be the turning point in their lives, offering a new way of being. Some students referred to IAIA as the place "where I was born."

I then began to wonder what the new National Museum of the American Indian could do to help the process along. And while I agreed with one of the museum's goals of helping in the preservation of Indian culture, I hoped that this did not mean some kind of cultural embalming process wherein obsolete cultural ways are kept going beyond their time. My idea of "conservation" or "preservation" means that the museum should take impeccable care of patrimonial objects in its collection. But a more important task should be that of using the objects in its care to help Indian culture develop new ways to respond to the dynamics of an ever-changing social environment.

I shudder when I hear people say that a museum's function is to "preserve the arts," seeing in my mind's eye someone trying to stuff artworks into a Mason jar. It seems to me that the preservation and conservation responsibilities of the museum are a given and that the real mission of the museum goes beyond being a place of cultural show-and-tell. The primary purpose of the NMAI should be to continue gathering objects related to Indian patrimony and devising ways to enhance the lives of living Indians.

People and cultures — like any living organisms — have to adapt to environmental changes; those that don't, die. The relationship of the past to the future has been stated in many ways — I like the declaration that "the future lies in the future, not in the past." As a generic institution, the museum has been more inter-

ested in digging up than in planting. Indians have long been denied access to their past, and now with the swing of the pendulum, they risk being denied access to their future.

The NMAI should develop vigorous, ongoing, blockbuster exhibitions of the finest traditional objects and activities of the past, combined with the finest current visual and performing arts productions. Such shows should be representative of the works of native peoples from this hemisphere; they should also be designed to show Indian truths to the world in a manner never afforded them before.

As I worked, admiring my selection of superb Northwest Coast hats, I wondered what it would take to help Indians today to reach the quality of human expression that the hats represented. In my ruminations, I found myself reinforcing long-held beliefs that the arts have unique powers to help people see themselves at their greatest levels of cultural and social development.

Art is an affective process; it deals with the deepest emotions and with the ways people feel about themselves and their environments, both past and present. I venture to say that more major life decisions are based on how people feel about things than what they know about them — the affective versus the cognitive.

Many important and positive developments are taking place in the lives of Indians today as a result of an increasing understanding of how to reconcile the lasting values of the past with the needs of modern life. But all is not well. There is palpable evidence that many Indians — suffering from decades of prejudice, oppression, and virtual cultural genocide — distrust the system and take refuge within the comfortable memories of their own cultural institutions. And while this attachment to the old ways is understandable, the reluctance to change is maintained

FIGURE 11
HAIDA HAT.
WOVEN, PAINTED SPRUCE ROOT AND CARVED, PAINTED WOOD,
HEIGHT 44.4 CM. (15.4313)

FIGURE 12
HAIDA HAT.
WOVEN, PAINTED SPRUCE ROOT, HEIGHT 34 CM. (5.5018)

at the cost of social mobility — even within the cultural setting they would like to return to. One cannot help but wonder at the resultant level of social and political disempowerment: severe levels of poverty; the dearth of available jobs or other ways to earn a living; high rates of alcoholism; estrangement of generations within the family; and other attendant ills.

I believe intensely that Indians, who have managed to survive for some thirty thousand years, have much greater strength than seems apparent today, but that these strengths have been submerged by overwhelming historical circumstances.

My appreciation for the beauty of the Northwest Coast hats that I have chosen to illustrate my views inspires me to think more about the role of the arts, both as mirror and goad, in the lives of Indians as they go about the reshaping of culture.

Observe what is happening to traditional ceremonies across the country. Most Indians live in urban communities and have long ago lost real touch with their home cultural bases. The pan-Indian powwow is a growing phenomenon that helps to make up for the loss of contact. Some of the most beautiful Indian arts of today are found in the costume developments going on at powwows, which also foster a continuing reliance on the drum. In this context, new dance forms have evolved, partly traditional, partly innovative.

Some communities successfully revive dances not performed in decades, while other revivals fail, and vital links to the past are lost. The changing lifeways of Indian youth and the decline of native languages threaten old religious traditions and general cultural stability, in spite of the revival efforts of a strong nationalist movement. Much of indigenous culture was originally linked inextricably with older religious patterns. Religion may

soon become increasingly ritualized, with culture more and more dependant on the arts to retain its distinction.

Observe the trends in music, with the intrusion into traditional drum music by new forms perpetuated by cowboy-type folk singers, rock groups, modern composers, and concert flutists. Watch how traditional Indian dance forms are moving to the stage as a new form of theater. Note the advent of new drama groups, playwrights, and actors.

Trace the disappearance of the tipi as a metaphor for changing lifestyles. Its loss comes just as it has gained worldwide admiration as an example of unusual architectural ingenuity.

Notice the lessening emphasis on traditional applied-art forms, which have served Indians for centuries, in favor of a growing fine arts movement devoted to art for art's sake.

Consider the fact that the making of Indian art for individual satisfaction long ago supplanted the production of arts and crafts for home tribal use. Consider the fact that the sales of Indian arts and crafts now run into the millions, and in many communities serve as the major economic mainstays. Note the rise of the individualist as artist, as opposed to the tribally directed artist of old.

Listen to the rumors of the imminent move of Indian designers into new production fields, such as the textile arts, fashion design, and household fabrics. Note the appearance of Indian architects and the ways in which they are adapting Indian philosophy and form to the creation of efficient living machines for modern society. Take stock of a stunning renaissance in Southwest pottery design and production.

One can only conclude that Indian culture is already using the arts to find its ever-changing new forms. This is very much in keeping with the spirit of traditional Indians, who have been adapting to changing environments for thousands of years. To Indians, the saying that "art is life and life is art" is but a cute phrase to explain what has been known for aeons.

SELECTIONS/FASHION

The Indian sense of beauty and design can serve as an inspiration to artists from anywhere in the world. One of the strengths revealed in Indian objects is that native artists were great fashion experts. People say that fashion is not very important, but I think it is one of the most basic of human enterprises. From day one people have cared about their appearance: "What do I wear today? How do I look?" It doesn't matter whether they are just going down to get a bucket of water or participating in an important ceremony. From tattoos to earrings to clothing, fashion is a fundamental form of expression. So I thought it would be interesting to explore that aspect of the collection. Moving in that direction, I discovered the Northwest Coast hats and came to see them as metaphors for human accomplishment.

I'm sure the people who wore these hats had some con-

FIGURE 13
HAIDA HAT.
WOVEN, PAINTED CEDAR BARK, 30.5 X 16.5 CM. (6.9255)

FIGURE 14
HAIDA/KLINKWAN HAT.
WOVEN, PAINTED SPRUCE ROOT, 38.1 X 16.5 CM. (2.1485)

cept of how they looked in them — they're so deliberately designed. And they're very contemporary. In terms of shape, form, design, and decoration, they transcend time. Modern painters would be fascinated by these hats for a variety of reasons: exquisite placement of design on the hat, simplicity of shape, and richness of color (figs. 13, 14, 15). Together they create a sense of harmony. I'd like to live in a village designed to look exactly like this group of hats. I'd like to live in a hat! They have a sense of beauty, shape, color, design — all the aesthetic requirements are there.

If we could reproduce in the Indian world the kind of life in which these hats had a place again, it would help restore a sense of dignity and importance among native peoples. If a native person today could wear such a hat with the same aplomb with which the creators of these hats wore them, I think you would see many contemporary problems vanish. So I see the hats as a symbol of something from the past — the hats evoke the beauty and understanding of that earlier life. They convey a sense of pride and of beauty — what that could do for new generations of Indian people would be fantastic!

FIGURE 15
TONTA/TLINGIT HAT.
WOVEN, PAINTED SPRUCE ROOT, 41.8 X 17.8 CM. (9.8095)

A renowned Ojibwe canoe-maker, **Earl Nyholm** is recognized as a significant cultural resource in his own community. Co-editor of *Ojibwewiikidowinan: An Ojibwe Word Resource Book*, a seminal work in Ojibwe language studies, Nyholm has also been a participant in the Smithsonian's Folklife Festival. Examples of his work as a canoe-maker are among the collections of the National Museum of American History.

In his visit to NMAI, Nyholm centered his attention on Ojibwe bandolier bags as masterful evocations of Ojibwe culture. Painstakingly created and beautifully designed, the bandolier bags suggest the patience and sense of artistry that, in Nyholm's view, characterize the Ojibwe people.

"How are we going to convince the younger people today to recapture that patience required to make a bandolier bag? When you make a bag like this, you put yourself into it, and it becomes a part of you. It's a two-way process. You sleep with it. You live with it."

EARL NYHOLM

· 49 ·

BEADWORK'S FINEST HOUR

The bandolier bag is the apex of Woodlands beadwork. If you wanted to take one item that personifies Ojibwe culture, it would have to be the bandolier bag, which not only exemplifies the state-of-the-art beadwork that the Ojibwe are known for, but also embraces the very idea of Woodlands culture in the prevalence of flower and fruit motifs.

These bags represent an era — they evoke a certain high point of the entire culture, an element of glory before decline set in. There was a definite pride that these people had that went from community to community, a commitment to not do anything that didn't measure up to the highest standards. The period before the so-called Pan-Indian movement, which started to hit Indian country sometime after World War II, was beadwork's finest hour.

Each bandolier bag, which could take as long as a year to make, represents an exceptional accomplishment. The making of a bag might have been a family project — or at least one between mother and daughter — that would require a great deal of patience. The effort could also involve taking time away from a lot of chores and other family needs.

Although women would wear them on occasion, the bandolier bags were primarily male attire, and every respectable Ojibwe man had one. For the women who made them, it was a labor of love, almost like giving birth to a child. It's also a little like counting the years by the rings on a tree you've cut down. One of these bags would be like a ring in a woman's life. Just to make one bag would be a year off her whole life.

The beauty of these bags has such high impact, it is unfortunate that you just don't see them anymore. They are so dramatic that a book or an exhibition should be devoted solely to bandolier bags.

THE PACE WE LIVE AT NOWADAYS

There's been a decline for many years — since about 1940 — in the quality of beadwork. After the forties, the desire to produce something as time-consuming as a bandolier bag seems to have declined. So many tribes had them, and then all of a sudden,

AMIKONS (OJIBWE), IN
TRADITIONAL DRESS WITH BANDOLIER BAG, 1923.
LAC DU FLAMBEAU, WISCONSIN.
PHOTO BY H. SMITH. (P10343)

· 50 ·

FIGURE 16
OJIBWE BANDOLIER BAG, CA. 1890.
BEADED CLOTH, 97.8 X 31.8 CM. (23.9923)

FIGURE 17
OJIBWE BANDOLIER BAG.
BEADED CLOTH, 82 X 35.9 CM. (19.3217)

bingo, nobody was making them anymore. Maybe it has something to do with the pace that we live at nowadays. We have lost much patience for doing things in the old way.

In their day, the bags were considered a part of proper dress, in much the same way that a man might wear a necktie or a woman a long gown for a formal occasion. Some of them have a little pocket in which people could put things; so, they're kind of a combination apron and decorative article for use at a ceremonial powwow or similar occasion. Back in the thirties — and even earlier, to the 1890s — these items were very proper. A respectable person wouldn't be seen without one, maybe even two. They wore them crossways, one on each side. I've also seen them worn in front, and I've even seen them on horses.

It would be interesting to trace the development, the history, of the bags. They seem to have been derived from the breechcloth and the woman's apron that were so common before the turn of the century; back then, every woman always wore an apron at home. I remember both my grandmas always wore aprons over their dresses.

INDIAN LOYALTY

There's probably no other ethnic group more loyal to the United States than the American Indian. That's ironic because this country hasn't been so kind to native peoples. Indians were not even granted citizenship until 1924. My grandparents refused to vote — they said, when we were young, we couldn't vote, so why vote now? In spite of all the abuse endured by Native Americans, we still love this country and often show that love in our art, as in the case of this bag (fig. 17). I usually think of flag designs as a novelty, but this example is not in the novelty category; it is extremely carefully made. It could be a signature piece. In the white man's culture, three and seven are the big numbers. In Ojibwe culture, however, four is the important number — there are four parts to your life, four parts to a tree, four directions, four layers in the sky. With this piece, there are four stars on each flag. This is a very beautiful piece of work — notice how the beads are placed so they don't interfere with each other.

Fourth of July celebrations continue to be important for the

OJIBWE WOMAN DOING BEADWORK
ON A HEDDLE. MINNESOTA. (P22761A)

Ojibwe. We would have a pow-wow on the Fourth, and back home in Michigan, we used to have a ceremony that was called the *Anishinaabe-niimi'idiwin,* a two-day or four-day dance. One of the first songs is the hand-shake song, then up goes the American flag, accompanied by the flag song. So for a lot of Indian people, the flag motif has significant symbolism.

THE DEFINITION OF "TRADITIONAL"

A lot of people use the word "traditional." I don't like that word. It's one of the most abused words in Indian-English today. In Ojibwe culture, we say that something has to be "proper," which means according to custom and whatever is necessary to make it correct.

When I was growing up, there were activities going on that people today would call traditional. But I didn't have that kind of realization. For example, we would camp out in the berry fields and pick berries. Or we'd go fishing beyond the trap line. That's all considered traditional. Doing beadwork, learning how to make canoes, harvesting the wild rice — all of that was just part of living.

Nowadays, they say that to

FIGURE 18
OJIBWE BANDOLIER BAG.
BEADED CLOTH, 122 X 33.7 CM. (19.657)

be a traditional Indian, you've got to go to so many powwows during the summer. Now, I remember my grandparents — I only saw them at two powwows, only two powwows, and I bet you my moccasin that up in Canada, there's some Indian people living up in the bush who are very traditional, but who have never been to a powwow.

THE DISTINCTIVE CHARACTER OF OJIBWE BEADWORK

When you look at Ojibwe beadwork, the most distinctive idea that comes through is this feeling of the Woodlands, the flowers; some bandolier bags also have fruit, such as grapes, depicted on them.

When you consider the bandolier bags that have the geometric designs, it becomes more difficult to characterize the nature of the beadwork, because without a doubt these geometric designs are much older. Even these geometric bags can be identified as Ojibwe, how-ever. Do you have a good imagi-nation? Can you see the geese in formation on this bag (fig. 18)? Geese are common in Ojibwe life. Even this tile-design bag (fig. 19) is clearly still Ojibwe — one of the clues, of course, is you've got the floral motif again.

Young kids back home would be able to identify the bags as Ojibwe right away because the patterns are indicative of our culture. But they wouldn't recognize the bag itself as a common item, unless they had been to museums and were aware of them. I think instinctively they would know that one of these bags is Ojibwe or Anishinaabe because of the character of the beadwork.

Some young people can look at this work and say, hey, my grandmother used to make these. But if we want to convince them of the importance of recapturing this lost art, they are first going to have to reexamine themselves — because we live in a time when we no longer have patience, and if you want to make something like this, that's what it takes, patience. Now we go into a fast food place to get our food. Years ago it took a while to make your food. Same thing with these bags. It took a long time to make them. How are we going to convince the younger people today to recapture that patience required to make a bandolier bag? When you make a bag like this, you put yourself into it, and it becomes a part of you. It's a two-way process. You sleep with it. You live with it.

FIGURE 19
OJIBWE BANDOLIER BAG.
BEADED CLOTH, 108 X 33.6 CM. (20.268)

SCATTERED CULTURE

When I make a canoe, I put myself into it, so to speak, and it's got to be a proper canoe. Many years ago, around 1975, a young Indian fellow, about fourteen or fifteen years old, expressed an interest in canoe-making. So he says he will go with me. See, when I make canoes, I start right from scratch, right out in the woods. All I take along is a saw and an ax and a knife, and that's it.

So we went out there. The young fellow lasted one week before saying, "Well, I think I'll go home." I asked him why. "This work is too hard," he said. I think sometimes you have to be a little bit older to appreciate an endeavor like this. He never returned, but now maybe he'd be ready to come back. I know there are certain young people who do have an interest in these things; years ago there was always a hardcore group in the community that carried on tradition, while others simply went along with the action, but we no longer have those people.

Ojibwe culture today is like a raw egg that is dropped and scattered, so all that is left is pieces. The pieces represent certain hardcore people throughout Ojibwe country.

If you could collect these carriers of tradition together in one area, then you could make the egg whole again.

When I look at art like the bandolier bags, it makes me feel proud because these things were made not so much out of a sense of obligation but because the people wanted to make them, and when you want to do something or make something, it takes on a greater meaning for you. Sure, there was a need for them, at the powwow or ceremony or whatever, but the degree of effort, time, and thinking that goes into these is something that can't be forced.

PERSONAL HISTORY

I think I'm an ordinary person, but maybe I do some things that are unordinary. There is a need inside me to do things the proper way. I didn't even know that I was a human being I think until I was about twenty-five years old. I didn't realize at that time that I was a real human being.

As an example of what I mean, here is a true story that I remember from a long time ago. There was an Indian boy whose mother was an Ojibwe and whose father was a white man. When he was about four or five years old, somebody asked him, "What are you anyway?" And that little boy says, "Oh, I'm half Chippewa and half human being." He was lucky. He figured out who he was real early, but it took me a long time. I didn't think I was a real human being.

I think there were a lot of contradictions in my life. For instance, when I went to school, the others used to call me chief — not a very good nickname to have. They would call every Indian a chief but, of course, they had no understanding of what it really means to be a chief. The people decide who will be chief. A few years ago I was with some friends in a restaurant in Michigan during hunting season. There were a lot of hunters from Chicago in this place. We were sitting at the table with our chief from back home, and this young fellow came over to our table and says, "I hear you are a chief." And our chief didn't say anything. Then the guy from Chicago says, "What makes you chief anyway?" And the chief says, "I suppose it's because I'm there when the people need me." The people made him the chief, and when they needed something, they went to him, and that's why he's a chief.

When I was growing up, everything was wrong. My relatives all spoke Indian at home. But when you go to school, you've got to speak English. When I was in seventh grade, I shot up to my present height — 6'2". You think I'm skinny now — you should have seen me then. It was incredible. I don't know what I weighed, but I had to wear snow shoes to take a shower. That's how skinny I was. And when I was in fourth grade I got measles. I also had to wear glasses, and nobody wore glasses then. Now it's fashionable. It turned out I was left-handed, too. So, nothing was right.

But those things that we did out there in the woods, picking berries and all that, that felt right.

I suppose some people do unusual things just for the sake of it, but I also think there are some people who are searching for something beyond the ordinary, because maybe beyond the ordinary you'll find that something that makes you "proper."

FIGURE 20
OJIBWE BANDOLIER BAG.
BEADED CLOTH, 66.1 X 19.7 CM. (20.1214)

Richard Milanovich is a member of the Agua Caliente Band of Cahuilla Indians in Palm Springs, California. Actively involved in preserving Cahuilla traditions, he has held a seat on the tribal council since 1977, serving as its chairman since 1984.

Milanovich believes that to appreciate the Cahuilla and other desert tribes of southern California, it is important to take into account the innovative and resilient spirit that has characterized their ability to adapt to, and survive in, a harsh environment. He sees the desert, the people, and their art as closely intertwined. In his view, this symbiotic relationship between land and people is integral to Cahuilla traditions and values.

"Indian people are more than feathers, they're more than paint. They are a deeply humanistic group of people who learned to live within their environment in a way that allowed an understanding of their environment and, therefore, of themselves."

RICHARD MILANOVICH

· 59 ·

MUSEUMS TODAY

I feel it is a crying shame that there are not more Indian people involved in museum work today. I go to a lot of different museums because I'm interested in history, but I never see Indian people working in the important museum areas — administration, curatorial, exhibitions. I think NMAI represents a good opportunity to get Indian people involved in museum work.

I don't want to take anything away from the non-Indian people who work in museums today. I think they're doing a marvelous job. But they do not have the same understanding, the same feel for artifacts or objects from Indian country. They're not Indian and as a result they can't understand all the nuances. Whether it's an exhibition display or the administration of collections, non-Indians proceed from a point of view that is foreign to us because they don't have that understanding. I'm not slighting them, but I feel that there should be more Native Americans involved, particularly with Indian collections.

There should be Indian participation from the beginning, to allow the native people themselves to discuss the issues or make recommendations as to how an exhibition should be constructed and what should be exhibited.

I hope that visitors to the museum will leave with the understanding that Indian people are more than feathers, they're more than paint. They are a deeply humanistic group of people who learned to live within their environment in a way that allowed an understanding of that environment and, therefore, of themselves.

People are too wrapped up in themselves today, whereas Indian people have a way of thinking in which the overall objective is to live a good life, a spiritual life.

SACRED OBJECTS

Ceremonial, religious, or sacred items are those that neither I nor any individual has the right to say should be displayed — the right to make decisions as to what can be exhibited must be bestowed by the people.

Care must be taken if an object has some religious, cultural, or sacred bearing about it. There are, for instance, medicine bundles in the museum's collections from two different tribes in California. There are also rattles and eagle-feather skirts. These objects are unquestionably of great beauty, but the significance behind them must be taken into account. I do not have the right to say, "Let's show these to outsiders."

Indian people do not want outsiders to know of their ceremonies, which in southern California we call "doings." These doings are not for those people to know. Throughout history, Native Americans have chosen a select few individuals to conduct ceremonies. They did this for a purpose, and I am not one to violate that tradition. Sacred or ceremonial items should not be on display.

REPATRIATION

If the museum is aware that a particular item has some cultural, sacred, or ceremonial significance, it should be returned immediately to the tribe it belongs to. The tribe should not have to make requests over and over for the return of sacred items. It is the museum's responsibility to return those items to the right people and let the tribe or tribal organization decide what to do with them. The museum has qualified individuals who know that certain items are sacred. They should take it upon themselves to return those items to the people.

CAHUILLA WOMAN PREPARING ACORNS FOR GRINDING.
CALIFORNIA. (P501)

MISSION INDIAN HOUSES, 1917.
MARTINEZ, CALIFORNIA. PHOTO BY E.H. DAVIS. (P682)

CAHUILLA MAN AND HOUSE, 1917.
PALM SPRINGS, CALIFORNIA. PHOTO BY E.H. DAVIS. (P2332)

There's a medicine bundle, for example, in the collection from the Soboba. I bet those people don't even know it's here. I'm going to go back and tell them that they can find it among the museum's holdings.

There are also human remains stuck away in closets and drawers in the Smithsonian. In California's state parks there are more than eight hundred Indian remains. In different facilities throughout the country, the National Park Service has human remains and grave goods that should be returned. Naturally, now that this new law [the Native American Graves Protection and Repatriation Act of 1990] has been passed, we will attempt to get them returned.

I'm sure there are ceremonial objects, grave goods, or sacred items that cannot be repatriated because the people to whom they belong have been victims of extermination — either through natural causes or government forces, which happened a lot — and are no longer around. But those items that cannot be returned should be set aside in a special area, where Indian people together can somehow decide what to do with them.

Let the decision come from the spiritual leaders. Let them determine how best to solve that problem. Don't allow some museum administrator to say, "Well, I know this is the best thing for them because I went to school for twelve years and I know what should be done." They don't know. Only the Indian people know what has to be done.

CAHUILLA HISTORY

Cahuilla means "powerful ones." We were a great and powerful people, as were all the desert people. We're still a proud people.

Our nation is comprised of seven bands: the Agua Caliente, Cabazon, Torres, Martinez (now combined as Torres Martinez), the Santa Rosa Band, the Cahuilla Band, and the Soboba Band.

There are tribal members who are able to speak Cahuilla — a derivative of the Uto-Aztecan language; in the area surrounding our reservation, there are a lot of people who still speak Cahuilla.

In the past, one was chosen to lead or to be a shaman of our tribe by the shaman or the tribal leaders, who would see a special quality in an individual as he was growing up. That was how the selection came about. It wasn't hereditary, but based on your innate abilities. It's not like that today.

We still have our clan system today. I am a member of the Coyote Clan. Bobcat and Coyote are the two animals that represent the four clans. The clans enable you to know where you come from, and it's still that way today. Clan affiliation is not talked about a lot, but when it comes time to vote, boy!

At present, there are 284 members, with 163 voting members, of the Agua Caliente. We have a tribal constitution and by-laws, which were adopted in 1953. Our council is able to make decisions for the reservation. We don't have to go to all the people for their vote. I have been chairman of our five-member council for going on ten years, having first come on the council in 1977.

The Agua Caliente Reservation consists of thirty-two thousand acres. We have a unique relationship with Palm Springs. Regarding development on the reservation, final appeal rights rest with the tribal council. In other words, the city processes development plans but if a council member or a developer is not pleased with what the city council does, they can appeal to the tribal council and we can overrule the city. Five times we've overruled the city completely on development plans. Twice we've modified and once we upheld the city on a decision.

INDIANS OF THE DESERT

There are other tribes in southern California that are listed as federally recognized (at the same time, there are thousands of Indian people from Los Angeles up through Yosemite who have not received federal recognition). Among the tribes of southern California are the Cahuilla, the Cupeno, Diegueño, Kamia, Quechan, Serrano, Mojave, and the Chemehuevi. We all lived as one within the desert. We could not have done it alone. We had to depend on each other for foodstuffs and various other goods that we were not able to produce ourselves or adapt from what was available to us.

So we lived through other surrounding peoples — tribes, individuals, groups. We were all one. Indian people, however, have done this throughout the country. They didn't just live off the country, they lived with it. In looking at the museum's holdings from this area, I want to show that this work is not just Cahuilla, or Luiseno, or Degenea. It's everything, everybody. This is the desert. This is the desert. All of this came from the desert.

Too many times in the past the California Indians, particularly the southern California tribes, have been somewhat overlooked because of the fact that we don't have a lot of feathers, we don't have a lot of fancy dancing. We don't have the material things — the big log houses, for example, of the Northwest peoples.

But we were able to survive in a land and in an environment that was difficult and harsh, and we continue to do so.

LEARNING TO ADAPT

We originally came down from the Great Basin in the Nevada/Colorado region, probably because of the over-population of the Great Basin. So we moved into an area no one thought was habitable. But it turned out to be quite livable.

We consisted of small groups of people living in a very unforgiving environment. Initially, we lived very simply — you have to learn to survive before you can enjoy it more. But after a period of time, we began adding beauty to our everyday life. You can see this, for example, in the basketry — especially the rattlesnake and the tortoise designs in the baskets.

We fully adapted to local foods — mesquite and cactus, for example. There are over fifteen types of edible cactus. The cactus buds or flowers are still used today. We even consider them to be delicacies now because not many people know how to prepare cactus. In addition, there are over 150 different types of plants, in an area about one-half by one-quarter of a mile. We also had beans, including a very sweet-tasting mesquite bean that we called our candy. We made use of the palm seed, the seeds in the gourds, and the beans from the Palo Verdi tree. Acorns too are a very important part of our diet. One of the dishes that's still made today when acorns are available is called *weewish*, which many of us still truly relish.

Our oral history goes back only five hundred years. So, we

FIGURE 21
DIEGUEÑO SANDALS.
LENGTH 28.1 CM. (8.2185)

FIGURE 22
CAHUILLA POTTERY JAR.
HEIGHT 40.8 CM. (21.8397)

weren't in this area for a long period of time — we weren't that fortunate. We were a relatively young tribe that had to first learn how to live within our environment. It took a long time to develop the wares from the resources that were available to us. But as time went on and we learned to survive and adapt, we also learned ways to enhance the basketry and other goods — by concentrating more on the visual beauty. Because the desert is a beautiful place. Once people come to the desert, they begin to understand what the desert actually means; they start to perceive the beauty in the desert. It isn't just all cactus and sun. It's a marvelous place to be.

SELECTIONS/AESTHETICS

Some of the design work on these objects — the arrowhead in particular — didn't become widespread until these items became popular. Indian people began to realize that the more designs on a basket or *olla*, the more commercially feasible that object became. At that point, the use of more elaborate designs became popular. Prior to that we didn't use ornate design all that much.

No reason or logic dictated the particular designs on the gourd rattles (fig. 23). The design was whatever the maker of the rattle wanted to portray. The rattles were used in our birdsongs and bird dances. The songs and dances are part of our oral tradition, through which we have passed on the stories of our creation. They're our wake songs and social songs. Unlike many other tribes, we didn't have drums. We had the gourd rattles.

✖

Olla is Spanish for earthen jar. The small mouth on this one indicates it was probably used to hold water (fig. 22). It is very utilitarian. Later, certain ollas were decorated. I do not want to show a decorated olla because these were normally used for ceremonial purposes and I am against the display of these objects.

✖

Burden nets, made from milkweed, were used to carry an olla, a wooden mortar, or possibly even a stone mortar (fig. 24). Some gathering and hunting areas were far away from any habitation site where we actually lived for any period of time. And there

· 67 ·

FIGURE 23
CHEMEHUEVI GOURD RATTLE.
PAINTED GOURD WITH WOODEN HANDLES.
LENGTH 28 CM. (11.6840)

weren't always stones or boulders readily available, so you had to carry the implements with you. We carried them with us to process the food on site rather than bring back the seeds or acorns — why bring back the shell if you could husk it on top of the mountain and bring just the meat or the pulp back?

✕

This rattlesnake basket, probably used for storage, illustrates how we moved away from the undecorated basket, as our skills developed and we had more time to appreciate what was going on around us; the objects evolved, with more decoration characterizing everyday life (fig. 25). Again, many of the more decorated objects were used for ceremonies or giveaways, and even for the commercial market after the 1890s, when such markets started becoming a way of providing necessary resources.

GIVEAWAYS
If a person or group of people accumulate more than their surrounding relatives, friends, or tribes, you would have a giveaway, during which the people would get together and share. Today's powwows or fiestas — especially when people come a long distance — often feature

FIGURE 24
CAHUILLA BURDEN NET.
189.5 X 108.9 CM. (7.1169)

giveaways. The host group or individual are the ones who give — to assist those who travel in order to participate in doings. It is a way of sharing to disperse some of the wealth that has accumulated. It's very important in all Indian communities as a means of getting away from the materialism so prevalent in contemporary society.

THE WAY I GREW UP
I wish I could say that many young people are interested in learning our language, traditions, or culture. Some are definitely interested but I can't say that this interest is prevalent.

I am hopeful that this national

museum will be a cultural center and will help us teach our children who they are and where they came from. We don't have that right now. Back in the 1950s it was believed that Indian people were not happy with themselves. It was a bad time for a lot of Indian people — Native Americans didn't like the idea that they were Indian. My mother was like that. And that's the way I grew up.

It was very hard for me back then — my family was ostracized for being Indian. I could see this bias and I could feel it going on all around me, but I didn't know what it was. My generation grew up in that time, when it wasn't good to be Indian.

Now people of my generation are trying to restore the pride of being Indian and pass that pride along to our children. I hope we'll be able to do it and I hope this new museum will be able to help us.

Indian people don't like to talk about themselves. They don't like to tell what happened before. They don't like to tell the stories. But now they're beginning to. They understand that Indians of my generation are attempting to bestow upon our younger people the knowledge that we did not have but which is so important to Indian people: Let us discover who we are.

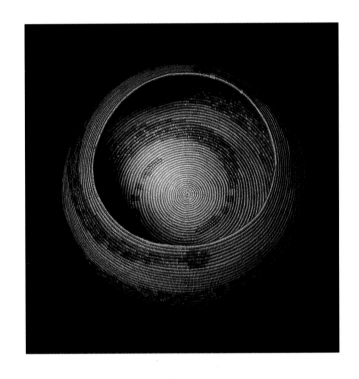

FIGURE 25
CAHUILLA BASKET WITH RATTLESNAKE DESIGN.
35.8 X 17.3 CM. (24.7735)

An accomplished dancer, artist, and teacher, **Edgar Perry** (White Mountain Apache) is director of the White Mountain Apache Cultural Center at Fort Apache, Arizona, and a former member of the board of trustees of the Arizona Historical Society. He has devoted his adult life to researching and studying Apache history and culture, establishing along the way a significant photographic and oral history archive. Perry was a contributor to NMAI's *Native American Dance: Ceremonies and Social Traditions* (1992).

Showing the diverse beauty of Apache traditions was Perry's primary concern during his visit to the museum: "We are gathering the wealth of things worth remembering," he says. He was especially interested in calling attention to Apache objects of everyday life.

"Kids today think the world has always been marked by TV, McDonald's, skateboards, football, basketball, rodeo, nice clothes, beautiful house, convertible, nice shoes, fancy saddle — all of these kinds of things. But I say to them: 'No, it wasn't always like that. We came out of the wickiup. We lived very simply. We slept on the floor, on the grass.' And they don't believe it: 'You're kidding!' they say."

EDGAR PERRY

· 71 ·

TO EDUCATE AND LEARN

I respect my culture and all of our Apache traditions. I believe we've got to keep our culture going.

My grandparents were very traditional people, and when I look at these objects from the museum's collection, I see my grandmother and grandfather in them. It's like they have left these behind. And that really means a great deal to me.

It is worth remembering where you came from, what you are, who you are — this helps ensure your future. And this is how I regard the *All Roads Are Good* project — we are gathering the wealth of things worth remembering. Along with our own experience of life, we can utilize this wealth for our children and for those who don't know about the Indian heritage. We're proud to have this culture, this rich heritage.

I have genuine respect for the people who have preserved and catalogued the museum's collections. I know that knowledge of Apache culture is limited, but I am sure that we can work together and do justice to the Apache artifacts in the museum. In the future, I would welcome an exhibition with videos, maybe music, and labels done phonetically in Apache. There is so much material for us to work with.

When you're a kid you take so much for granted. There are so many things I remember from childhood that I wish I had saved. But now they're all gone. We used to have a lot of photos in my mother's house. I asked her what happened to all those photographs and she said that they just disappeared. We take so many of these precious things for granted — we don't take care of them, or we give them to somebody, or sell them off cheaply.

I feel comfortable working with these objects. When the people back home ask me about this project, I tell them that I'm

WHITE MOUNTAIN APACHE WOMEN AND GIRLS
PLAYING GAME IN FRONT OF WICKIUP, CA. 1900. ARIZONA.
PAUL WARNER COLLECTION. (P17564)

WHITE MOUNTAIN APACHE CLIFF DWELLING, CA. 1900. NORTH
FORK OF WHITE RIVER, WHITE MOUNTAIN APACHE RESERVATION,
ARIZONA. PAUL WARNER COLLECTION. (P17577)

just trying to educate and learn. Kids today think the world has always been marked by TV, McDonald's, skateboards, football, basketball, rodeo, nice clothes, beautiful house, convertible, nice shoes, fancy saddle — all of these kinds of things. But I say to them: "No, it wasn't always like that. We came out of the wickiup. We lived very simply. We slept on the floor, on the grass." And they don't believe it: "You're kidding!" they say. They watch television and listen to the radio. There's maybe one hour of traditional White Mountain Apache songs on the radio, but it's very little. Our children go to school where English has always been taught, and everything is computers, typewriters, and business. They have to read a lot of books, and everything is in English here — our radio station, television, magazines, and newspaper. They don't see Apaches in any of these things.

DAAGODIGHA

The literal translation for *Daagodigha* is "they will be raised up." It is the name given to a religious movement dating from 1903 to 1907. Daagodigha, begun by a White Mountain Apache religious leader named Daslan, spread among several White Mountain Apache communities. The followers of the movement were to partake in a series of dances that were going to lead the people up into the clouds, while the old world was destroyed and a new one created. The leaders of the Daagodigha movement instructed their followers to dress a certain way — moccasins, white dresses, and white shirts, for example, were items of clothing associated with the movement. The medicine man who started Daagodigha wanted to have all his followers meet together on a hill. My grandfather, Scott Clay, said they wore long shirts that had the cross and crescent Daagodigha sign on the back. He said they

were all dressed in white shirts with vests, the medicine man's caps, and moccasins. Some of them also carried baskets and saddlebags with the cross and crescent design.

This movement was unique to the White Mountain Apache, and the people really believed it. They went through all the dancing and procedures required. It's very interesting now to look back on the movement. It's a beautiful history. It would be good for our people to bring back some of the things that happened in the past — it will raise questions, which in turn will bring out a lot of the older people and get them talking to the younger generation. People in their sixties, seventies, and eighties know a lot about Daagodigha — my mother, who is seventy-five, knows. A lot of the old people have so much to give, to share. They may not be able to read or write, but they have all the knowledge and the wisdom.

Daagodigha followers were supposed to be holy and pure. They prayed and sang, and the medicine man would sing, until it seemed like they were about to be lifted up. The people probably wanted to get as far away as they could from the white man, who was interfering with their religion and their culture.

APACHE TRADITIONS/SOME SELECTIONS

The Apache people used to move around frequently, looking for food. During the summer, they moved up into the mountains where there is a lot of snow — because when the snow melted, many herbs could be found. During the fall, they would gather the food and go back down to a lower elevation, where it wouldn't be so cold as up in the mountains. During July they'd be looking for acorns in the lower country — like Wilcox and Tucson. Our summers are kind of short. We plant in April and harvest by August or September, after which the frost begins.

FIGURE 26
WHITE MOUNTAIN APACHE MOCCASINS.
DEERHIDE UPPERS, COWHIDE SOLES, GLASS BEADS,
AND SINEW, LENGTH 41.2 CM. (16.7349)

We didn't have very much in the old days. We made a lot of big baskets and really depended on them because we didn't make pottery. We used baskets for a lot of survival and personal possessions. Moccasins, too, were very important. Some moccasins have uppers made from deerhide, with the sole from cowhide. Before the use of cowhide, they used hide from the neck of a deer, which was thick and good for the sole. The distinctive, round toe of the moccasins protected the toes from sharp cactus, rocks, sticks, snakes, and other dangers.

Our people are very religious and some of our moccasins have crosses on them (fig. 26). When we're walking on the holy ground, in God's country, we dance with the moccasins on. Most of the beadwork is made by the women, but sometimes the Apache men do it. The people know they've got to get ready for certain special times. In the old days the people would get everything they needed together and make preparations. We didn't have a clock or anything — we just went by the seasons. When a girl becomes a woman, for example, we make moccasins for her. Moccasins have a vital role. The first thing you do when you get up is put on your moccasins, so you're ready to go. If your enemies are nearby, you're prepared to jump and go. And when you put on the moccasins, you do the right foot first and then the left in a clockwise fashion that shows respect for Mother Nature — that's Apache tradition.

✖

In the old days, the Apache man would be blessed holding his lance, *ikage* (shield), and bow and arrows before he went to war. Everything would be blessed for the purpose of bringing the man back from war. They would decorate the shield with the medicine man's designs. Shields were very special.

I know this shield is telling us something but, with all the symbols of the medicine man, the true meaning lies somewhere back in the days when it was created (fig. 27). It means a lot of important things: prayers to bring the shield's owner back, and protection so that bullets won't go through him and arrows will ricochet off the shield. That's what they did to protect the warrior.

✖

FIGURE 27
WHITE MOUNTAIN APACHE SHIELD COVER.
DEERHIDE AND PIGMENT, DIAM. 47.6 CM. (18.4403)

FIGURE 28
WHITE MOUNTAIN APACHE HAT.
DEERHIDE, EAGLE FEATHERS, AND GLASS BEADS,
23 X 47 CM. (9.4071)

The four cardinal colors — the east is black, the south blue, the west yellow, and the north is white — can be seen in this hat (fig. 28). This hat also shows four things that hold great significance for the Apache: the eagle feather, turquoise, deer thong, and the yellow pollen. Each individual Apache has an eagle feather that has been blessed by the medicine man for each person when they were young. The eagle feather is for protection and must be kept with us wherever we go. A turquoise stone is for boys and a white bead is for girls and women — these represent the power of the earth. The deer, representing the power of the animal world, is very sacred. For Apaches, the deer is an object of prayer and respect. The deer, a source of clothes and food, has also been important for our survival. Yellow pollen represents the power of the water world, and is used to pray and bless with. All these sacred items must be together with you at all times.

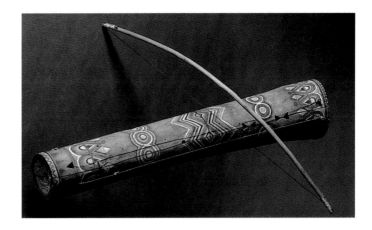

FIGURE 29
WHITE MOUNTAIN APACHE *NADAH BENAGOLZE* (VIOLIN AND BOW).
AGAVE, PIGMENT, AND BALING WIRE WITH PAINTED DECORATION,
HORSEHAIR STRINGS, 67.3 X 16.6 CM. (20.7147)

APACHE MUSIC

Apache songs are never written — they're all handed down orally. Grandparents will teach children, maybe when they're deer hunting or acorn hunting. Many elements of Apache life are handed down like this through the generations.

Some songs are learned from medicine men inside the sweatlodge. Different medicine men have their own followers. The medicine man will get all of the people who are learning from him, and they will sing all the songs they are learning at a feast, or dance, or maybe a powwow. This kind of social event — where they all sing together, stay together, and follow the medicine man — is a good time to learn.

Sometimes, though, medicine men don't sing a complete song all the way through. They just sing highlights of their song, and then they cut it off. They'll sing only some of the verses, or start with the sixth verse instead of the first, that sort of thing. They do this so nobody will steal their song.

The Apache people use the drum all the time when we're singing to help keep the beat, the rhythm, going. The flute is for practice when we're alone. The wood that it is made out of is called *sool,* which is also the Apache word for flute. After Contact, the Apaches really liked metal and started using metal flutes. The Apache man who knew the songs would usually

know how to play the flute. Women sang too, so I imagine women would play it too, when they were alone, by themselves. The flute was for personal and private use, to keep people going.

The *nadah benagolze* (Apache violin) is made from the naturally dried stalk of the agave (fig. 29). We cut a section of the stalk off, split it, and remove the inside fiber, making it hollow. Then we put holes in it and decorate the instrument with Apache colors and designs — triangles and circles, and the four Apache colors (black, blue, yellow, and white). There's a little bow that goes along with it, and the strings are made from a horse's tail.

The notes go up and down with the turning of the pegs — tightening the strings makes the violin's tone go higher, and when you loosen them a little bit, it goes down. I think the violin would be kind of weak played at a social dance. But I don't know — in my life I've never seen anybody play the Apache flute or violin. Today, when we get together in a social dance, we usually have four drums and a lot of singers.

There are many people who don't know the songs. But they might know the songs of some of the famous medicine men because the music is still there, and they're still singing. And our music is played on our radio stations. The old people are still singing.

CROWN DANCE

When we do the Crown Dance, the clown appears first wearing the *Tulbaaye bich'ah* (clown headdress; fig. 30) and carrying a wand. The headdress represents the eagle, turkey, deer, and *gaans*, the mountain spirits who drive away evil. And the wand represents the thunder, the rain, or the lightning from clouds. He comes in with his bullroarer and wand to tell the people that the Crown dancers are coming. The bullroarer represents the power of the four winds. This is why the clown always goes to the four directions and whirls the bullroarer. He tells the people to make room and blesses the ground where the Crown dancers will dance. Then the Crown dancers will come into the dance arena or around the bonfire. At the end, the clown will make the last circle around the bonfire, whirling the bullroarer. The clown is very important in the Apache dance. Clowning can be fun, but it is sacred too. Clowns and gaans are sacred; they have the power to cure. A clown appears with four gaan dancers during curing ceremonies and during the Sunrise Ceremony, which prepares a girl for adult life.

During the curing ceremonies, the Crown dancers dance around the sick person, coming to him from four different directions, circling clockwise. The dancers tie yucca all over the sick person. The tying represents the sick person's pain. So, with their power, praying, and singing, the dancers then cut the yucca, which represents the person being released from the pain.

Before they make the clown's headgear, the men take a sweatbath together. They all go in together, and the medicine man sings. He sings four songs inside the sweatlodge. The boys hold the drum outside and beat it. Then when they go out the rest will go in. They go like that until everybody gets in. Many men work on the headgear. The clown's headgear, with just a cross, is easy to do and is made first. Then the other four headdresses are made.

THE FUTURE

Young people, like my grandson, have a strong feeling of wanting to stay and live on the reservation, and learn about their traditions. I've taught my grandson since he was three years old. He's a good dancer, and he makes his own headgear. Your grandkids want to do what you're doing — if you're an artist, for example, and doing a drawing, they'll say, "give me paper, I want to draw, too." So I'll say to my grandson, "Chris, could you help me with this? You can help me do this," and he does. He's a really good carpenter. He could probably make a violin. He helps the Crown dancers to paint the designs on the headgear. He's the first dancer because his headgear is big. He wants to make more, so I got a lot of materials for him — I got this bundle of sotol here ready for him.

He wants to learn Apache, and I speak to him in our language. There are a lot of kids who want to learn Apache. Their everyday language is English, but it's good to have both languages — then you can understand both sides. And it's best to learn when you're little because that's when it's easier.

Still, it's difficult; it will be a challenge for them. And that's where I come in — trying to help them with the phonetics and writing. What I want to do is record a lot of Apache, because the language is really difficult. When you say "grass," for example, you say *tl'oh* — and it's a clicking sound; it seems like it explodes in your mouth.

FIGURE 30
WHITE MOUNTAIN APACHE *TULBAAYE BICH'AH* (CLOWN HEADDRESS).
COTTON CLOTH, SOTOL, PIGMENT, AND SINEW, 55.4 X 45.1 CM. (9.4586)

Navajo weaver **D. Y. Begay** lives half the year on the Navajo Reservation near Chinle, Arizona, on land her family has occupied for more than a hundred years. The rest of the time she lives in Scottsdale, Arizona. Begay travels frequently, conducting workshops as far away as Australia. Her brilliantly colored textiles are characterized by bold, innovative designs.

For Begay, weaving is an integral aspect of Navajo culture, particularly for Navajo women. Begay, who stresses that Navajo weaving has historically been a "form of communication between tribes," is interested in weaving tools and textiles from other cultures. Her own love of innovation reflects the Navajo penchant for experimentation with techniques, materials, designs, and colors.

"Is Navajo weaving a dying art? I don't think so, because I work and talk with a lot of young women who are interested in weaving, and they want to learn.... I don't have any daughters but there are many Navajo women who want to learn and I want to share all the information that I have. I want to help preserve the art of Navajo weaving."

D.Y. BEGAY

· 81 ·

LIVING IN TWO WORLDS

I learned how to weave from my mother. She never told me specifics — like how many lines you have to weave or what to do when you want to weave an arrow — but the basics came from watching her. My involvement with weaving also came from my personal interests and experiences — taking fiber classes and reading books in high school and college increased my knowledge.

My mother is very proud that I have a strong interest in weaving. She is interested in what I have learned from reading books and talking with weavers of all kinds. She likes to hear about my experiences, such as teaching a weaving class for non-Navajos and traveling to other countries to see different types of weaving.

I did not express an interest in weaving when I was very young. I guess I took it for granted. My mother was always weaving. It wasn't until I was twelve or thirteen years old that I showed some interest in weaving. At that point, I started looking at weaving techniques, not just Navajo weaving but weaving from other cultural areas. In college I also became aware of different types of weavings. My experiences as a student really opened up a lot of doors for me.

It's important to know how to weave and how to deal with the process of weaving itself, from owning and caring for a flock of sheep, to shearing the wool and getting the materials together. Knowing that process involves looking at the weaving tools themselves. They're very basic tools, made from wood, and they are an important part of the weaving process.

My family has both sheep and goats, so I get some wool from my family. And I order some from the University of Utah, which is the site of a Navajo sheep project. I get wool from other sources too. I get some fleece from West Virginia. Wherever there happens to be wool, I'll try it!

I'd love to have three me's — to be wife, mother, and artist. It is really hard to juggle all those roles. It becomes even more complicated, because in a way I live in two worlds: in a traditional one, at home with my family, who speak only Navajo, and with my husband, who is Anglo. Of course, I respect his culture as well. It's a challenge, but I make the best of both worlds, going back and forth.

I want people to see Navajo weaving from a weaver's point of view. Weaving is a part of my culture and my heritage. I'm always asked the question: is Navajo weaving a dying art? I don't think so, because I work with a lot of young women who are interested in weaving, and they want to learn. I think it's very important to know how to weave and to know the techniques. I don't have any daughters, but there are many Navajo women who want to learn, and I want to share all the information that I have. I want to help preserve the art of Navajo weaving.

THE ART OF WEAVING

As a Navajo, a belief that is very strong in my heart is that being a Navajo woman means knowing how to weave, and how to deal with the process of weaving itself. I grew up with weaving. This

NAVAJO WOMAN WEAVING, 1897. CANYON DE CHELLY, NEW
MEXICO. PHOTO BY T.H. O'SULLIVAN. (P1743)

belief is a central part of my life. Incorporating my interest in weaving with this belief makes me an artist.

Although Navajo weaving is known nationally and internationally, few people have considered it from a Navajo weaver's point of view. Coming to the museum and looking at the materials here is a source of inspiration for me. It helps me to understand the actual process. I ask myself, who's going to come into the museum and view these materials? What are they going to think? These are important concerns to me because these materials represent a vital part of my heritage.

THE ROLE OF WOMEN
Navajo women are very important in our society. They are the caretakers, the ones who make the decisions. We are a matrilineal society: it's not that we don't respect men, but we grant women a more important role.

For women, knowing how to weave is intimately bound up with being Navajo. Most Navajo women know how to weave, but there are very few women who make a career of weaving. Because of this, most Navajo women would not claim to be expert weavers. Such a claim would violate their sense of modesty.

Nowadays, most women have their weavings set up in their houses, and they still take care of all their other obligations — getting their children ready for school, cooking, doing the laundry, running errands, and sometimes herding the sheep. And whatever additional time is available, they put to weaving. It's part of a woman's activities. Everything's just part of your life.

SOME BLANKETS
The early blankets were very basic and simple. I think that's why they are beautiful. These pieces are very important to me because I can go back and look at them and it helps me re-create images that I like. The early pieces that remain intact are an especially significant resource.

This blanket has been worn; it looks used (fig. 31). It gives you a good sense of the natural white and brown wool. The dyes are indigo and cochineal. This is an excellent study piece because of the colors, the basic and simple design, and the techniques. Pieces like this are foreign to Navajo weavers today, most of whom are probably unaware that these blankets have been preserved. We don't see these on the reservation and we don't go to museums or galleries. People in remote communities don't have access to books or other resources.

This piece is very old and it's been in the hands of many people who are not Navajo. It also could have belonged to a Navajo person now deceased. A Navajo might be reluctant to touch or see this piece. I know my mother doesn't like going to museums because she says the objects there are all about dead people; they are things from a long time ago.

✖

The wedgeweave technique fascinates me as a weaver. At one time Navajo weavers experimented with this technique, and most wedgeweaves were made as wearing blankets to sell. They are rarely exhibited, and most contemporary weavers do not practice this technique. This is a very exciting piece (fig. 32). The colors are bright Germantown yarns and the blanket has a perfect scalloped edge.

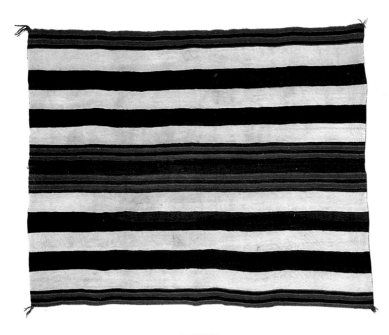

FIGURE 31
NAVAJO CHIEF'S BLANKET.
WOOL, 174.8 X 137.5 CM. (8.8038)

NAVAJO WOMAN CARDING WOOL.
VICINITY OF RAMAH, NEW MEXICO.
PHOTO BY PAUL J. WOLF.
(P15278)

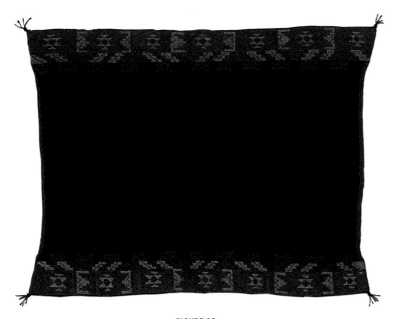

FIGURE 32
ACOMA PUEBLO MANTA.
WOOL WITH EMBROIDERED PANEL, 136 X 105.5 CM. (24.7827)

FIGURE 33

NAVAJO TWO GREY HILLS RUG.

WOOL, 179.9 X 113.1 CM. (24.1070)

Today most weavers sell their work. If you go to any Navajo family's dwelling you won't find a piece hanging. Even in the old days weavings were traded and sold to tourists. They were once used as clothing — wearing blankets and wool dresses — but now we only wear them on special occasions.

Rugs

Colonial influence throughout North America and the expansion of trading posts at the turn of the century actually enhanced creativity among Navajo weavers. Weavers studied designs that were foreign to their eyes and then elaborated on them, a process that inspired creative exploration and self-expression.

This rug tells the story of when the traders came to the Southwest (fig. 33). The rug is woven with handspun wool. That's important to me because spinning is a vital step in the weaving process. The woman who created this rug is not a novice weaver, because spinning this amount of wool takes a lot of skill and patience. Spinning looks very simple when you watch somebody

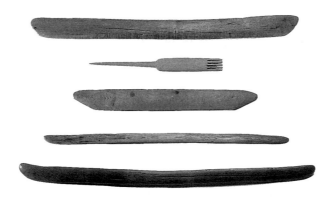

FIGURE 34
NAVAJO LOOM WITH WOOL BLANKET AND TOOLS.
113.1 X 104.2 CM. (19.3044)

doing it, but when you put it in your own hands, that's a different story.

Looms

This is the traditional way a rug was set up (fig. 34). The heddle is partially laced, the shed stick is present, and there are four different size battens, which show the progress of the weaving. You can see an excellent display of tools. The thicker batten shows a lot of use — teeth marks. The shorter, thick piece appears to be an addition to the set. The bottom warp beam is present, laced with cotton string. There are selvage cords. The heddle is pretty much intact and laced with cotton string. The top warp beam is present, and is completely bound to the warp. The outside frame is missing, as is one tension bar from the top.

Back in the old days, this loom was probably carried around. The weaver might have set it outside, using two trees as the outside frame. When working outdoors, you have the advantages of natural light and plenty of room. In the old days, a lot of the hogans were very small and accommodated a family of five or more people,

· 87 ·

so there wasn't much room to set up a loom inside. Weaving took place inside during the winter, but during the summer, a lot of women wove outside.

WEAVING TOOLS

I am very interested in weaving tools of all kinds. Tools are basic. I wonder what people thought about when acquiring or making tools. The men made the tools for the women; and I find myself wondering — what was he thinking about when he carved this little design? As an artist, I wonder — what was she thinking about when she wove a comb into a rug? They're all an inspiration. When I consider weaving tools, I go home with refreshed attitudes and ideas.

The weaver uses narrow heddle sticks as shuttles. When a weaver has only two inches left to weave, she removes her batten, heddle, and shed stick because there's no room to use them. Then she takes one of these very narrow pieces and uses it like a needle to weave.

✖

This is a very basic tool (fig. 35). It's a traditional Navajo spindle with the stick pointed at each end. It has some spun wool on it. You can tell that it is homemade, because the stick itself is not very straight. Today many people use dowels, shaping the tip and adding a spindle whorl.

YEIBECHAI CEREMONIES

This rug depicts dancers in a Yeibechai ceremony (fig. 36). During these ceremonies, the women are often invited to dance with the men. The men wear regular clothes on the first night of dancing, and on the second night they paint their bodies and wear moccasins, sash belts, cloths around their waists, and yei masks. The dancers depicted on this textile are not wearing masks, which means it is the first night of dancing.

We are not supposed to weave yeis, but it is often done today. I like this piece because the faces are almost real. Other yei rugs that I've seen are usually profiles of elongated faces; circles are hard to weave. But the shape of these faces almost makes them look real — the eyes and the mouth, and the coloring of the faces.

FIGURE 35
NAVAJO SPINDLE WHORL.
WOOD, WITH WOOL, LENGTH 57.1 CM. (24.7487)

FIGURE 36
NAVAJO YEIBECHAI RUG.
WOOL, 179.6 X 119.5 CM. (21.8703)

A multimedia visual artist from the New Mexico–Arizona area near Window Rock, **Conrad House** has lived and worked in many parts of the United States. Although his father is Navajo/Oneida and his mother Navajo, House says, "I identify myself more with Navajo." His work has been influenced by the cultures and aesthetics of many different tribes — with beadwork, pottery, and Crow Indian artwork all playing a part. He has most recently worked in glass sculpture.

House feels a passionate need to bring the pride and dignity of his people to light. As respectful as he is of traditional beliefs and customs, he thinks it is important to call attention to contemporary Native American art as one way of indicating that "life is still going on — our culture is not dead."

"How you live life is both an art and religion, as is how you treat and respect the environment — including animals, plants, and fellow humans — all life forms, even our Mother Earth. We see no need to create concepts to separate or fragment our daily lives. You need not have to go to church and pray when your home and environment are your church, your place of prayers. Try to live a clean, beautiful, good, and balanced life. Be generous and caring. That's what our elders tell us."

CONRAD HOUSE

My Own Art

I'm an artist. I do what I do – if you want to place labels on me, that's okay. But when it comes to calling me a printmaker, ceramist, bead-maker, glass-worker – I stay away from that, even though I work in all those different media. I'm a multimedia artist. I even sing and dance.

I've always been influenced and interested in the world's cultures, especially Native American cultures. My Haida and Tlingit friends have influenced me. I've also been influenced by the ancient pottery traditions of the Anasazi and by contemporary potters of Acoma, Hopi, Santa Clara, and other cultures of the Southwest.

In my "Chief Blanket" series, I incorporate the use of Seminole patchwork. I enjoy experimenting and incorporating various sensibilities in my creations. Freedom is essential to my creations.

Within the last four years, I've been doing a series of drawings and beadwork that rely heavily on Crow designs and color use, but without actually copying the original. The broad use of geometric colors had a soothing effect on me. Pink began to enter my color palette more (fig. 37).

✕

Traditionally, Navajos (Diné) are matriarchal. Women have considerable control over various matters – livestock, land, wealth, and children. I come from a family of strong women – my grandmothers, my mother, my aunts, and my sisters. In my black drawings and collage work, I honor and acknowledge their strengths. With the broad use of black and cochineal red, I refer back to the traditional "bil" dresses woven before calico came into vogue.

The Display of Sacred Objects

Navajo people, to this day, are very protective of our culture and the information that we let out. Because of our teachings – the teachings of our grandparents and mothers and fathers – a lot of this sacred material is still ours. Some of the things in the museum, like medicine bags, we believe should be returned back to the earth. And throughout the museum's collection I've noticed that the medicine bags of a lot of other tribes are tucked away, suffocated in plastic. Actually, when I first came here I thought there would be whole boxes filled with Navajo ceremonial objects. But that's not the case. The holdings are very limited, which is actually good in a way – because our grandparents and the grandparents before them were very protective of the sacredness of these objects. And that belief is still alive. It lives in me. In other cultures maybe these beliefs are dwindling away, maybe others are giving up, or selling their ceremonial objects. But many of us still believe and protect our beliefs.

Many of our traditional people would be afraid of such sacred objects. It could be dangerous. They would say that it should be returned back to the earth – our mother. Some things should not be seen. I respect our traditional way, but part of me understands the need to preserve our past in museums, as a way for people to know and understand our existence. Such preservation is a way for the coming generations to see who we were and who we are.

FIGURE 37
CROW BEADED MOCCASINS.
HIDE WITH GLASS BEADS, LENGTH 24.2 CM. (11.8008)

NAVAJO WOMEN CARDING WOOL.

(P19919)

In order for our people and other people to understand our beliefs and the sources of our culture, we need to see these things, to let them be out there. These objects are for our people to hold on to; they are our secrets.

Most medicine people would not even come to a museum and handle another medicine man's bundle. They would say that it would be dangerous. You have to be cautious and careful and need to know the songs and knowledge before you open a *jish*, or medicine bag.

At the museum, I saw a number of sacred masks covered up with plastic. In our way, this is wrong. The masks have got to breathe because there's energy in them — in the Navajo way, they're alive. You can't suffocate them or they'll be angry in time to come. You always bring them out to breathe. Museums always put things in plastic. The older people would be really firm about this kind of thing. They would get mad about anyone opening things or showing things, or even sharing certain kinds of information. The older people are much more protective of that knowledge. Because we are going through a time of constant change right now, a lot of our younger Indian people have misused the imagery and the meaning behind these sacred objects.

Some of the younger people don't respect the traditions. They would probably just open the medicine bags, with no feeling of guilt or reverence. But I come from a family that respects the Navajo way. It is part of our life and reflects how we were raised.

Today many of our historical and sacred sites are being in- truded upon and threatened not only by outside invaders, but even by our own people. Non-natives are overwhelming our very existence, affecting our water, air, and land. We must continue to protect ourselves in an era of greed.

With the problems of over-population, we see an increasing number of non-natives looking for free souvenirs. As a result, we find a number of our historical and sacred sites being overrun by souvenir-hunters — those very people who are insensitive to our indigenous cultures — looking for "Indian artifacts."

One of the only ways to know and learn about the sacredness and significance of these sites is by living within your culture: living, talking, eating, and sharing with your relatives and people. It is through this kind of interacting that a culture survives and exists. There are many knowledgeable people familiar with traditions.

I know too many natives who have to do research to find out who they are culturally. It's a sad state of affairs when people must go through the library to find out about themselves. We must be participants within our community. I know too many natives who talk about the beauty of nature and traditional life, but who live away from their respective cultures. How is a Navajo raised in New York City going to find out about the wonderful smell of sage or cliffrose?

NAVAJO PEOPLE SITTING IN FRONT OF SHELTER.
(P21214)

Navajo Traditions

First of all, I want to say I am not an authority on Navajo traditions or culture, and do not speak for all my Diné people. What I know is information that I have deciphered myself throughout the years. There is an endless amount of information out here on the Diné reservation.

Traditionally, we have four main clans and from these derive many sub-clans. We come from different areas, so therefore we all have many different experiences even though we share the same culture and land. There are many clans that trace their origins to a pueblo, tribe, or even a people, such as the Mexican Clan.

Our Diné traditions have changed over the generations, but there has always been an important underlying belief that has carried us throughout the centuries — and that is the need to maintain balance and harmony with the world around us, especially the natural world. This reverence for the earth and all life forms is evident among indigenous peoples throughout the Western Hemisphere, from Tierra del Fuego to Barrow, Alaska.

While some cultures preferred and valued (and even waged war for) the shine and glitter of gold, diamonds, rubies, emeralds, and sapphires, not to mention spices, our material culture was closely connected to the earth. Even in the taking of material there was a reverence for the material, apparent in the practice of asking for permission and giving thanks.

Throughout the generations, from our ancestors to our people today, we still prefer the beautiful turquoise, white shell, abalone, and obsidian — sacred, hard materials representing the directions, seasons, and cycles of our life.

It is through the arts that our culture continues on and survives. It is through some of the cultural materials that we see our traditions and beliefs — our world view.

Most Diné know that what is important and necessary to one's well-being is balance and harmony with oneself and one's surroundings, and especially with the natural order of things — Mother Earth and Father Sky. It is through ceremony that we bring back balance and harmony.

What represents this balance, harmony, and wholeness, we can see in this Diné basket (fig. 38). It holds our world view. It has the opening to the east and the rainbow band encircling.

FIGURE 38
NAVAJO BASKET.
PROBABLY UTE- OR PAIUTE-MADE. 12.5 X 40.5 CM. DIAM. (20.8372)

Designs of clouds, mountain, red evening sunset, night sky, white dawn, and the seasons are indicated on that band. It suggests the ups and downs of life spiraling around — cycles.

✖

The basket is a necessary component in most ceremonies or "sings." The making of these baskets also must be done in a prescribed way to be ceremonially functional or acceptable (fig. 39). For the most part, the technology of basket-making has remained the same. The only difference is perhaps the use of various hues of red with the use of commercial dyes from purple to bright red.

Weaving is an ancient tradition in the Southwest. The Diné have a reputation of excellence in the realm of textile arts. It is from the pueblos that we incorporated this important art. Traditionally, the Diné women did most of the weaving. Textiles represented wealth and industriousness. Diné blankets were highly prized trade items among many tribes and pueblos. Now they are mostly a source of income. Most commonly we now see the Pendleton blanket at all social functions. Commercial fabric now is also used in ceremony as an offering or payment.

When you go to a Navajo wedding or puberty ceremony, you see a lot of blankets hanging on the wall, making it very festive (fig. 40).

✖

When I was growing up, many of my relatives were weavers. One of my aunts, Gladys Taliman, specialized in the "Chief Blanket" style. It was simple in composition compared with all the elaborate and complex designs we see today. As I began to see more chief blankets, I saw the strength and boldness of that style in black and white bars and vibrant reds. How brilliant and regal it must have looked a long time ago to see people in the desert country riding to a ceremony — the reds, indigo, and the stripes!

After seeing NMAI's collection of chief blankets, my interest and inspiration have been sparked even more. I did a small beaded version. The use of space, color, and even texture fascinates me.

It should also be pointed out that before weaving, the Diné valued various animal hides — weaving and hides were in the same category as "soft goods" used as presents, payments, and

FIGURE 39
NAVAJO MARRIAGE BASKET.
PROBABLY UTE- OR PAIUTE-MADE. 8.5 X 35.4 CM. DIAM. (11.5490)

FIGURE 40

NAVAJO BLANKET.

WOOL, 202.5 X 152.3 CM. (10.4303)

offerings during ceremonies. Native tanned deerskin is also a necessary component in many important sacred ceremonies. Buffalo, antelope, and elk were also highly prized. In old times, one way to show off your wealth and demonstrate that your husband was a good provider was to have nice deerskin leggings — no holes, tanned, soft, and bone white was most preferred.

During a ceremony, it was important to dress "traditional" so you could identify yourself to the *Diyin Diné* (Holy People) and to all the natural elements — the mountain, corn, clouds, for example — whose help you are asking in maintaining your balance and harmony. You would have your blanket, moccasins, jewelry, pollen bag, and headband if you're a male.

Sandpainting — dry painting with colored sand, flower petals, pollens, etc. — is an art form that many people associate with the Diné. These paintings are very restrictive and have many rules that one must abide by. They are done ceremonially to bring harmony and balance.

Today we see the commercialism of sandpainting as a form of income. Many traditional Diné are opposed to this because it only promotes imbalance and confusion. Now you even see the "End of the Trail" sandpainting being sold. I don't see myself or my Diné Nation as being defeated or being without hope, or even becoming extinct. Again, we are changing, growing, and surviving; despite the pressures of the dominant society, we remain uniquely Diné.

Throughout the Diné arts, it should be noted that there were unique individuals called the *Nadle* who carried the knowledge and creation of these arts. Some of the best weavers were Nadle.

Even the invention/discovery of such lesser-known arts as water bottles, pottery, and grinding stones were associated with the Nadle.

THE NAVAJO CREATION STORY

All life forms originated from the earth and the union with the sky. There are a number of different variations of the Diné creation story, but I know most mention the evolution of our people from four previous underworlds: the black, the blue, the yellow, the white. Now, today, is the fifth. Some people say this is the glittering world. When I see the shiny glass, metal, and plastics around us, I know what they are talking about.

In the black world of darkness, thought and dualities were established — female/male, for example — and order was growing. In each world, conflict arose through imbalance and disharmony, jealousy and adultery, so each time the people escaped to the upper world and each time they met different peoples — locust, swallow, deer, and so forth. At that time, animals and insects also made their way up each time, all assisting our ancestors. We were not in the form we are today.

These stories are too long to recount, but as we evolved and developed, order was being created by the Holy People: first man and first woman and other beings — animals of all sorts, including man — understood and could communicate with each other. We all grew and evolved together.

Each clan has varying creation stories, so I can't speak for all the Diné. There are many different clans. But I belong to one of the four original clans, the *Kiyaa'a'anii* ("The Tower House People," related to the ancient Chaco Canyon/Anasazi culture of the Southwest).

We were created from Changing Woman, who represents the seasons and the earth. She gave us the bear to protect us. One story goes that we were created, with the assistance of the wind, from two perfect ears of corn, white and yellow, laid on the skin of a ceremonially killed deer. It is in our fingerprints that we see the evidence of the wind.

BALANCE

According to the old stories, the previous worlds that existed show that we were out of balance four times, maybe more. A lot of that imbalance came about because of our own doing — jealousy, envy, adultery, greed, incest, and so forth. Even though there were warnings and signs saying be careful, beware, the people just didn't listen. But there's always that group that will listen, that will hold the old ways, that will treasure them, respect them, revere them. As time went on, four worlds had to be destroyed through floods, fire, disease — almost like the plagues of the Bible — before we came to this world.

But we evolved, we grew. And the cycles will always continue on and on, forever and forever, like the seasons. There will be a time of disruption and chaos, and out of that comes order, as indicated in the Navajo basket.

What I see reflected in the bars on Navajo blankets is that simple symmetry, that balance. The idea is that we should try to live in balance with the world, so you have balancing elements and beautiful elements. What you strive for in this world is *hozho* (beauty, balance, harmony). How you live, how you treat one another, the way you cook, how you arrange your home, how you live in your surroundings — in the Diné way this would be art and religion.

How you live life is both an art and religion, as in how you treat and respect the environment — including animals, plants, and fellow humans — all life forms, even our Mother Earth. We see no need to create concepts to separate or fragment our daily lives. You need not have to go to church and pray when your home and environment are your church, your place of prayers. Try to live a clean, beautiful, good, and balanced life. Be generous and caring. That's what our elders tell us. Think good thoughts. Pray. Don't disrespect that anthill over there. Don't go killing all those crawdads. Ever since I was a child, they always told us these things.

THE OLD WAYS

The knowledge of traditions and culture is carried on by our *Hataŧi* elders. Their purpose is to ensure our health and balance. Many Hataŧi are known for certain ceremonies or a number of ceremonies. They are our healers — doctors, astronomers, herbalists, and so forth. The literal translation of Hatahłi is "chanter," or "singer." It is through songs that our origins and relationships are recited; it is through song that we express our life — like laughing and crying.

When we were growing up, one of the only connections we had with our past was through our relatives and parents. Our schools were really lacking — we were taught to be like the white people. They never even mentioned Navajo history. It's better nowadays. Navajo history should be taught, even in white history classes. We need more of our own culture to be brought back to us in our schools. Museums should facilitate our access to collections that have been hidden away from us.

THE FUTURE

I would like the museum system to meet the Indian people: take their collections to the reservation. Show us the good quality works, the old works our people have been separated from for so long. Museums hold that. What I would like to take back to the reservation is the idea, the energy, that is needed to identify ourselves, to maintain our identity. To know who we are and where we're coming from so that we can have a foundation for our future. And that belongs to our children. We need to take back to the reservation many things. We need to get the young people rejuvenated again, make them proud of our uniqueness.

Life is still going on; our culture is not dead. It lives in us. The mediums I work in are very non-traditional, but they hold a lot of the traditional images and beliefs. Museums aren't only places where old buckskin, old objects, are preserved and displayed — eventually they're going to have to start collecting material objects that we make today as contemporary Native Americans. There is a gap between the old museum stuff and what we're doing right now. There's a void in between; there needs to be a way to show the connection between the object in the museum and what is going on now, a sense of cultural progression. Because ours is an ongoing, living culture.

Emil Her Many Horses (Oglala Sioux) lives in Chicago, where he is studying to be a Jesuit priest. As former director of the Buechel Memorial Lakota Museum on the Rosebud Reservation in South Dakota, he helped develop an arts and crafts co-op, which now has more than two hundred members. An artist himself, he concentrates primarily on beadwork.

Visiting the NMAI collection evoked pride in Sioux history and traditional values for Her Many Horses. He viewed his participation as a selector as an opportunity to find answers to his "questions about ancestry" and to help educate his people about the accomplishments of earlier Sioux leaders and artists.

"There seems to be a great resurgence of interest in the old ways. People are going back to the traditional religious practices.... Younger people are attending *yuwipi* ceremonies, purification ceremonies, and learning songs. People are going back to their relatives, or their ancestors, to try to find any information they can."

EMIL HER MANY HORSES

· 103 ·

YOUNG MAN AFRAID OF HIS HORSE
(OGLALA), 1879. PINE RIDGE RESERVATION,
SOUTH DAKOTA. (P4025)

THE OLD WAYS

I'm a person filled with questions, and I viewed the opportunity of looking at the artifacts in the NMAI collection as a way of answering some of my questions about ancestry. I have wanted to do some research on the early days of my people. The saying that comes to mind is, "To know the future is to know your past."

There seems to be a great resurgence of interest in the old ways. People are going back to the traditional religious practices. Throughout the summer, for example, several Sun Dances are now sponsored at Pine Ridge, Rosebud, and other reservations. Younger people are attending *yuwipi* ceremonies (usually conducted by a medicine man), purification ceremonies, and learning songs. People are going back to their relatives, or their ancestors, to try to find any information they can.

What is happening today reminds me of what went on during the early 1860s when leaders like Spotted Tail, Crazy Horse, and Young Man Afraid of His Horse were all part of a renaissance of the warrior societies. The Sioux people had become dependent on rations from Washington and on a variety of trade goods. And as a result, they had to go back and relearn the old ways — how to hunt buffalo and engage in military strategies, for example.

CRAZY HORSE AND OTHER CHIEFS

Crazy Horse was one of the Sioux "shirtwearers" (councilors) from the Oglala tribe. A few years ago, I attended a conference where a slide of this shirt was presented and I was overwhelmed when I saw it at that time — I didn't know this shirt existed (fig. 41). One of the reasons I chose this shirt was so that other people would know about it and be able to admire it. Crazy Horse was a very brave person, and this shirt symbolizes his personal dreams.

At the time that the elders picked Crazy Horse to be a shirt-wearer, our people needed leaders from among the younger men. Crazy Horse stood back in the crowd when they named him as a shirtwearer, but the people made a loud trilling noise, which was a sign of approval or honor. Then he came forward in a humble way.

FIGURE 41
CRAZY HORSE'S SHIRT.
OGLALA LAKOTA. HIDE WITH PAINT, SCALP LOCKS, AND
WOODPECKER FEATHERS, LENGTH 84 CM. (16.1351)

FIGURE 42
SPOTTED TAIL'S SHIRT, CA. 1855.
BRULÉ LAKOTA. HIDE WITH PIGMENT, SCALP LOCKS, QUILLWORK, AND BEADS,
LENGTH 81.5 CM. (17.6694)

I believe that at that time about four shirtwearers were named to lead the people and the warriors. This movement required that the people revive a lot of the old ways to survive, and they needed leaders to do that.

I remember doing some research on this shirt, and when I saw it, it prompted these stories in me. What I hope is that it will prompt other Sioux people to look back in history to these older warriors, or chiefs, and consider our heritage.

✖

As with Crazy Horse's, I don't believe that people know that Chief Spotted Tail's shirt exists (fig. 42). Chief Spotted Tail was from the Brulé or Sicangu Sioux, one of seven different branches of what are referred to as the Teton Sioux. This shirt is heavily decorated with a really unique technique of quillwork.

Chief Spotted Tail brought the Jesuit missionaries to educate the young people of the tribe. As a result, on the Rosebud Reservation today, Chief Spotted Tail has come to symbolize education. The community college there is named after him.

One of the stories that this shirt prompted in me is from the book *Crazy Horse* by Mari Sandoz. She recounts how Spotted Tail was in battle during that time; unarmed, he charged the enemy many times over. During the battle, his wife stood on the hill making trilling noises — supporting her husband while he was in combat.

I think the scenes depicted on the robe of Young Man Afraid of His Horse, another Sioux shirtwearer, probably represent his various exploits (fig. 43). The hairdo, the clipped hair up front, suggests Young Man Afraid of His Horse must be fighting Crow Indians.

Even today we have some chiefs who wear the shirts that are referred to now as "Chiefs' Shirts." Today's versions are much longer and are done with beadwork. Certainly someone who was named a chief would have the right to wear one of these shirts.

BEADWORK
When I was in high school, I saw some beadwork that I wanted, but I didn't have any money to buy it. So I thought, well, how do you do it? Eventually I learned how to do it from a couple of

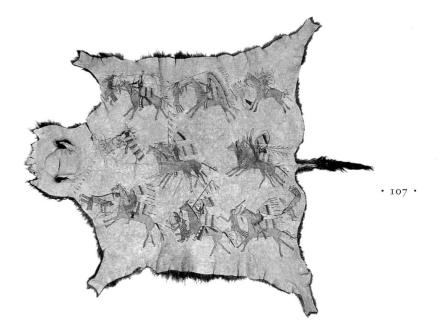

· 107 ·

FIGURE 43
YOUNG MAN AFRAID OF HIS HORSE'S BUFFALO ROBE, CA. 1880.
OGLALA. PAINTED BUFFALO HIDE, LENGTH 223.5 CM. (522)

SIOUX GIRL WEARING A DRESS WITH FULLY BEADED
YOKE, PROBABLY CA. 1890S. PINE RIDGE, SOUTH
DAKOTA. PHOTO PROBABLY BY GRABILL. (P22896)

people back home. One of the people who taught me was Alice
Fish, an older lady who did a lot of beadwork. She was very good
and I could go and talk to her.

One time my sister wanted a fully beaded dress. So I went to
Alice Fish and said, "How did you make it?" So she got a piece of
a regular, brown shopping bag and took out her scissors. As she
was talking to me, she started folding and cutting the paper.
Then she showed it to me and said, "This is where the design
goes." It was just amazing. I took the pattern she made home
with me and cut it out of leather. When Alice would do a design,
she would just draw a pattern right on the material and then do
the beading.

I made a beaded cradle once with horses on it; the horses
were styled after those made by one of my great-grandmothers.
She often did the horses in red, yellow, white, and shades of
blue. I once asked my dad about it because he spent a lot of time
with his grandmother. "Why would she use all those various
colors?" I asked him. He told me that she probably did it to
represent the four directions. Sometimes back home, the colors
that represent directions are different according to different
medicine men. West is usually black, that's fairly common for
Sioux. But the other colors sometimes change. He said that
sometimes blue was substituted for black. With the particular
medicine man that my family followed — black is west, north is
red, east is yellow, and south is white.

�֍

This is a "box and border" robe done with beadwork (fig. 44).
Originally, this type of woman's robe was painted. This particular
robe may have been made either for a "giveaway" or to bring a
person out. I was especially interested in choosing this particular
piece because, before I came here, an artist back home named
Dorothy Little Elk expressed an interest in reproducing one of
these pieces for a competition, a beaded box and border hide.
She asked me how they were made and I was able to show her
some old photographs. When I came here and saw this robe, I

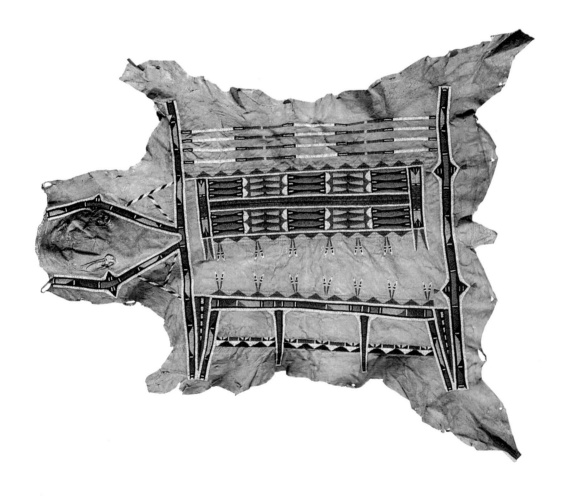

FIGURE 44
SIOUX BEADED DEERSKIN.
115.5 X 185 CM. (11.1739)

wanted to pull it and look at it right away.

✖

This parasol could have possibly started out as a novel item that someone made for herself in the early 1900s (fig. 45). It is done in what's referred to as the Eastern Sioux style — with abstract floral beadwork. It's made with cut beads and also with some floral-style quillwork.

This is a style that not many people are doing today, which was one of my reasons for selecting this piece. My grandmother talked about how her grandmother could do this floral-style beadwork. She once had a pattern book with various patterns in it; it would have been great to have that book. But she said that her grandmother could bead like this, in the floral style. This is an excellent example of both beadwork and quillwork. It's made of soft, tanned hide, probably deer.

GIVEAWAYS

You hear stories today about people who would take off a fully beaded dress right there at a giveaway for their loved ones — they had several calico dresses on underneath — and give that very elaborate work away.

FIGURE 45
TETON LAKOTA PARASOL.
BUCKSKIN WITH QUILLWORK AND BEADS,
58.5 X 64.5 CM. (12.2259)

After the reservations were established, a lot of things were produced for giveaways. I know my grandmother has stories about "celebrations" (social gatherings) that were held on the Fourth of July. A red (copper) penny was given to each person selected to be on the organizing committees for these dances. If you received one, you would have to come back a year later to acknowledge the honor of being on the committee. They would sing what were called "penny songs," which evolved into today's giveaway songs, to honor relatives.

Today, blankets are a popular giveaway — either a commercially produced Pendleton blanket, which is a woolen blanket with geometric designs, or star quilts with different color and starburst design combinations.

INDIAN VALOR

I remember a story that my uncle told me about a man named Has Many Wolves As Friends, which was translated later as Plenty Wolf. Plenty Wolf was taken prisoner by his enemies, and later escaped from them. He had a ball and chain on his foot, however, and the

SIOUX CAMP SCENE, CA. 1890.
PINE RIDGE, SOUTH DAKOTA. (P22851)

way he got back home was by carrying that ball. I don't remember when this was, but my uncle said that when Plenty Wolf got back to the reservation, he told his family members that he had to carry the ball and chain and that sometimes he had to crawl, dragging the ball with him. His relatives started crying and they made a song about his escape. It was a personal song that told the story of his bravery in the face of adversity.

Such songs are common among all native people. For example, there were quite a few people from back home who ended up going over to Vietnam. They volunteered and went over there to fight. When they came back home, the people had honoring powwows for them. And throughout the time that they were over there, the families back home all got together in their honor. Vietnam veterans, or any veterans, are honored like that. There are certain veteran songs. A wounded veteran usually gets a red eagle feather to signify his valor.

Indian people are such forgiving people; this trait shows up a lot. In spite of our history, for example, many Native Americans have great respect for the flag, and American Legion posts are very strong among native peoples.

· III ·

Gerald McMaster (Plains Cree) was born and raised on the Red Pheasant Reserve in Saskatchewan, Canada, but has written that "I've been an urban Indian since the age of nine." Trained as an artist at the Institute of American Indian Arts in Santa Fe and the Minneapolis College of Art and Design, and as an academic at Carleton University, Ottawa, McMaster is the curator of contemporary Indian art at the Canadian Museum of Civilization in Hull, Quebec.

McMaster's ecumenical perspective on Native American cultures found its sharpest focus in his response to native footwear. The museum's large collection of moccasins and other kinds of footwear became a metaphor for the diversity and creativity of indigenous peoples.

"I was very sad when I first saw these objects because many of them have left their homes and are no longer with the people. This made me see immediately the ruptures in Native American history, including our art history. Through these exhibitions, and through the repatriation process, however, many of these objects are now making those connections again with the people — they're going back home. So, that feeling of sadness is slowly leaving me."

GERALD McMASTER

· 113 ·

PAIUTE MEN IN TRADITIONAL DRESS.
KAIBAB, ARIZONA. (P107)

Connections with the Past

All Roads Are Good is an examination of the kinds of objects collected by the museum's founder, George Gustav Heye, during a period in history when Native Americans were believed to be vanishing. Heye amassed more than one million artifacts, primarily in the twentieth century, although many of the objects date from the nineteenth century. The collections demonstrate the tremendous creative diversity and craftsmanship of Native American peoples. This project is a testimony both to our connections with our ancestors and to the vitality and perseverance of the Native Americans who have survived. The Native Americans who have participated in this project have tried to rekindle the spirit of connection with our ancestors. The project's title suggests the idea of perspectives — that everyone's perspective comes from a point of knowledge, a point of understanding — and we hope non-natives will bring not only their own perspectives, but a desire to learn more about ours.

The project shows that many Native Americans continue to persevere and remain vitally involved with their cultural identity, through which we are building connections to the global community. *All Roads Are Good* is also a result of the kinds of work that museums have been doing over the past hundred years; in particular, it indicates the kinds of changes in the art world that have led museums to work more closely with Native Americans.

Looking at the objects during my time here has been a tremendous learning experience. Not only have I learned about some connections I have with my own tribe, but I began to enlarge my sense of the objects Native Americans have been creating for hundreds of years. Yet my initial impressions were ambivalent. I was excited when I began looking at the objects — many of them

I had never seen before, although as a young student, I was familiar with a number of books on the collection and knew that many of the objects had become famous in Native American art history. But I was very sad when I first saw these objects, because many of them have left their homes and are no longer with the people. This made me see immediately the ruptures in Native American history, including our art history. Through these exhibitions, and through the repatriation process, however, many of these objects are now making those connections again with the people — they're going back home. So, that feeling of sadness is slowly leaving me. Although knowledge of some of the objects will be forever lost, I feel optimistic about the kinds of programming, which will be certainly guided by Native Americans, planned by the museum.

In Someone Else's Shoes

I came to this process as a curator and artist, and I wanted to be able to combine the two. I didn't want to be so tribally-specific as some of the other selectors. I wanted to be able to draw upon the museum's vast collection and look at objects that came from all parts of the Americas. That was when I had the idea to explore moccasins and other footwear (fig. 46). "Moccasin" comes from the Cree, or Algonquian, word *maskisina*, meaning shoes or footwear. It is a generic term, unlike the narrower meaning it is given today.

My original intention, which we later scaled down, was to show a mile of moccasins — to illustrate the old truth that to understand somebody else, you have to walk a mile in his shoes. We discovered through computer searches that the museum's collection contains more than two thousand different pairs of moccasins. If you consider the wider definition of footwear — taking into account all the types of footwear worn by the indigenous peoples of this hemisphere — there are many more than five thousand such objects in the collection. So, lined up one in front of the other, with each shoe approximately one foot long, the total would be close to one mile.

Moccasins have another advantage in the selection process — they generally do not fall into the category of the sacred or sensitive. They belong more in the secular plane (although some researchers and experts might suggest that some moccasins are indeed sacred, in that they may be used in special ceremonies; these cases are rare, but all precautions were taken in the final selection). Footwear tends to be more neutral — it is not as politically sensitive as other objects. There is also a sense of movement inherent in footwear — in fact, I wanted to display these objects in a circular fashion, so it looks as if the moccasins are performing a Round Dance.

By using footwear and the cliché of walking a mile in someone's moccasins, I was able to address the idea of multiple perspectives, which is so central to this project. The moccasins also provide an immediate sense of the vast quantity of objects in the museum's collections, since these objects emanate from so many different culture groups. The footwear offers a sense of what native cultures were at one time. This was a chance to make a hemispheric statement about Native Americans, one that suggests the connections between our ancestors and the Native Americans of today.

Today we take great care with the kinds of shoes that we wear, and it was no different in the past. Native Americans, particularly the women, took great care with the materials they selected in making footwear. The shoes themselves have an expansive range and we find very different kinds of footwear — from the north we have sealskin-covered shoes that are approximately knee-high and probably stuffed with some very warm materials; while down through the Woodlands and to the Plains we see footwear that covers the foot and ankle; and in the open desert area of Mexico we find that sandals are preferred. There is great diversity not only of shape, but of materials. Some scholars have suggested that the aesthetic of the shoe was self-directed; in other words, the design faced the wearer. You will notice this in the Plains and Woodlands styles. No doubt the aesthetic of all this footwear will appeal to the sensibilities of contemporary New Yorkers, but I would hope Native Americans first take a very careful look.

The moccasin itself was the perfect shoe to wear, as it conformed to not only the shape of our feet, but allowed our feet to conform perfectly to the contours of the land. Within this vast city, the moccasin in some sad way evokes our yearning for nature, for the land, and our need to touch the earth once more. The moccasin allowed us to touch the earth, whereas the shoes we wear today shield us from the concrete, and the concrete in turn shields us from the earth — so we are doubly removed from the earth's surface.

As we begin to re-articulate our cultural identities, lifeways, values, and beliefs, Native Americans must realize that objects such as these moccasins are more than a reflection or representation of the past — they are products of the past that point to the future; they signify the potential that exists within our communities. The objects speak to individuals, families, tribal groups, students, and scholars, and help to define our humanity on the earth.

FIGURE 46
MOCCASINS AND OTHER FOOTWEAR FROM THE NMAI COLLECTION
(SEE P. 224 FOR ACCESSION NUMBERS)

FIGURE 47
TETON LAKOTA DANCE STICK.
PAINTED, CARVED WOOD, LENGTH 89 CM. (14.1566)

Other Selections

My interest in the "horse sticks" was in the qualities of sculpture apparent in the way the artists who made these objects perceived form — yet they tied the form inextricably to the complexities and drama of ceremony and meaning (fig. 47). These are sculptural pieces on the one hand, while on the other they carry tradition.

With some of the other objects I looked at — a number of the spoons, for example — I was struck by how powerfully simple they are in their shape and design (figs. 48, 49). I think we can look at them from that aesthetic perspective. And as I looked more closely, I began to see other possibilities — the connection with food, for instance. Food and eating call to mind giving, protection, and feeding, which in turn suggest a connection to Mother Earth. Food is symbolic of Mother Earth because it comes from the earth. So these objects can take on a more cosmic significance. I can't really say anything about the meaning of the animals depicted, unless they are in some way related to an individual.

FIGURE 48
SIOUX BUFFALO-HORN SPOON.
HORN DECORATED WITH QUILLWORK, LENGTH 21.4 CM. (15.8931)

FIGURE 49
SIOUX DOUBLE-HANDLE HORN SPOON.
LENGTH 20.3 CM. (9068)

I also looked at a number of bowls that are too culturally sensitive to illustrate. These objects have been empty for a century. But they still evoke a feeling of nourishing. They seem bountiful, intellectually bountiful. I think that somehow these bowls have to be filled once again, maybe this time around with ideas. The possibility that these bowls could nourish our grandchildren is very real for me.

The spoons and the bowls don't marry up directly, but I think they are connected in their simplicity — to me they carry with them a lot of information that is key to understanding how people responded to the world around them. The way these objects achieve their essence in abstraction is what is so wonderful. I think we should also try to discover the further levels of meaning and reference that derive from the addition of other materials.

✖

When I look at some of the sacred materials, something starts to come over me and overwhelm me. It's not so much because of the power that the object holds, but more what happened historically to native peoples. These sacred materials were denied use and function within their cultures because of outside intervention. When I go back to my own people today, a sense of the power these objects once had has now completely disappeared. I hurt inside when I see this because these materials could have been very powerful, yet today we have to conduct investigations to pick up information about them. Much of the meaning and power is lost and that causes me genuine sadness — that's the only way I can describe it. I feel for other native peoples who have lost their connection to these objects. With our tribe, there's very little left of sacred materials.

THE NOBLE SAVAGE

The image of the noble savage has had a tremendous impact on the way Native Americans are perceived. Through marketeers and others, this notion has entered into everyday consciousness and, in the past, influenced key nineteenth-century artists like George Catlin, Karl Bodmer, and Frederic Remington.

My interest is in the influence this image had on the artists and intellectuals whose theories about "Indians" were in part founded on it, as well as the ways in which the noble savage idea affected mass culture. In fact, I think popular and intellectual notions affected each other — artists like Catlin helped create the popular interest, stimulating a mass market for images of Indians, which the system then began to pump out.

A lot of clichéd, noble savage material is still out there; it continues to be mass-produced for large audiences. The image is popularized by both Indians and non-Indians. But there's also something very interesting about these images. For one thing, they're often well-crafted. I was in Denver once, looking in the antique stores and finding some interesting material — there was one gold plaque profiling an Indian wearing a headdress that I really wanted. It was absolutely wonderful, but too heavy for me

CHIEF BACON RIND (OSAGE), 1908. (P706)

to carry. What has begun to happen in the '80s and '90s is that Indians are reappropriating these images. Now, we are defining who we are and what this material is all about.

THE NATIVE SENSE OF QUALITY

I don't have a great deal of knowledge about old objects. My expertise is in modern cultural production. But it seems clear to me that many older objects display a very high sense of control, which begets quality. I think the high quality reflects the fact that the makers of these objects knew what they were doing, they understood their culture so well. When you know what you're doing, and when you know the meaning your work carries, all the elements work together. To me, the native sense of quality is imbedded and inherent in the notion of understanding the meanings of everyday life. Today we can make things of quality, but quite often the purpose of these things is unknown — they are just created and people like them. It is at this point that materialism starts to enter into the picture.

The notion of quality in traditional Native American cultures defines a different sensibility than what we are accustomed to today. These days, quality seems to be primarily a question of form. But quality is more than some merely formal dimension. It goes beyond that. The quality of traditional objects is so intrinsic to the work — it grows out of an understanding of the total culture, the intimate knowledge of the structures, the ecology, the layers of meaning within the culture.

Dancer and storyteller **Abe Conklin** (Ponca-Osage) is a leader among his people. Conklin, who is from Guthrie, Oklahoma, has spent his life immersed in the traditions of the Ponca. A veteran of World War II, he is an appointed leader of the Ponca Hethuska Society at White Eagle, Oklahoma, and was endorsed by the Ponca Council as their speaker and representative while visiting the museum.

Conklin stresses the spirituality and resourcefulness of Indian cultures. Mindful of the difficulty the Ponca have had retaining their traditions — among the Ponca, very little remains of older traditional material — he welcomed the opportunity to view the museum's collections. Although the museum's collection of Ponca artifacts is not large, for Conklin, it was "the most I've ever seen in one place."

"I look at these things as sacred objects. I don't look at them as just things — a legging, or shirt, or shield. That's why when I prayed today, I couldn't help but cry. Because I know that way back there one of our ancestors touched this object, and he might have touched it in a sacred way. It was a good feeling to know that I was able to see and touch something that some of our elders had touched long ago."

ABE CONKLIN

· 123 ·

STANDING BEAR (PONCA).
(P18029)

EVERYTHING WE DID WAS MADE WITH PRAYER

At the beginning of time, *Wakonda*, the Creator, sent out a bird — the spirit bird. The bird flew all over the world and then landed on the Ponca people. They say the bird was known as music, and that's why the Ponca made such beautiful music. This is a story that I've heard from many different people.

We never forgot our Creator because he's the one that made everything possible. If it weren't for him and Grandmother Earth and all of the spirits, we wouldn't be able to live. Every object that we made — from the smallest doll and the dice and dice bowls, to the leggings, shirts, and headdresses — was made with prayer. We prayed before we made any of these things, and a Ponca will tell you, "These were made with prayer." That's how religious our people are.

The only perfect person is Wakonda, so when the Poncas made something, they would put in an odd bead or in some way break the pattern so it wouldn't be perfect. This was to keep us humble — only God can make something perfectly.

I look at these Ponca objects as sacred. I don't look at them as just things — a legging, or shirt, or shield (fig. 50). That's why when I prayed today, I couldn't help but cry. Because I know that way back there one of our ancestors touched this object, and he might have touched it in a sacred way. It was a good feeling to know that I was able to see and touch something that some of our elders had touched long ago.

FIGURE 50
PONCA COAT.
HIDE WITH BEADS, LENGTH 71 CM. (3.6483)

FIGURE 51
OSAGE PIPE.
LENGTH 36.9 CM. (2.886)

The most important thing in the lives of Ponca people is our Creator. Our Creator comes first before anything else, and we look to him for understanding and wisdom, and for help to do the right thing. We turn to him first, and then we turn to our daily chores.

We are very religious, spiritual people. Before the introduction of Christianity, we had a good religion. We believe that our Creator is in every living thing on this Grandmother Earth. Everything we see in the world — birds, animals, even Grandmother herself — is a part of God. God has created all these things and he is within all of us.

I never did believe in the Christ from overseas. I tried to, but I just couldn't accept it. I knew the Creator had been working on me from the time I was little. I knew that we had our own prophecies, our own men. Don't get me wrong, I don't disrespect Christ. The way I look at it, he was a holy person who performed miracles across the ocean. We had the same kind of people here before Christianity was ever introduced to us. We had holy men who could perform

miracles as he did over there. We just lost one last December, Frank Fools Crow. He could heal people, the same way Jesus did. Many people witnessed his healing power. Even though I tried hard to make myself believe that Jesus was my savior, I could not. I realized he wasn't my savior, but the savior of those people across the ocean.

I DANCE HARD

I've been dancing since 1929, when I was three years old. I was received into the Ilonska with a sacred pipe that our people seldom use today (fig. 51). My sister Helen Bear said she remembered this ceremony. My grandfather took me to the sacred circle and presented the leadership with a sacred pipe, which was then smoked by all members. Tobacco was used in many different ways. If we went to visit another tribe, we sent tobacco to them first. If the tribe accepted the offering, then we came in as friends. If they sent the tobacco back, we left because it meant they didn't want us there at that time. They might have had something going on, like a ceremony, where outsiders weren't welcome.

FIGURE 52
PONCA DANCE BUSTLE.
135.7 X 45.7 CM. (3.6735)

✖

When I decided to become a dancer, I made up my mind that I was going to get recognition. So I watched all the men dancing my kind of dance in a contest, and I noted the dancers who won. Then I went to these old fellows and asked them to share their wisdom on dancing. I'd play the Ponca music tapes, with nobody around, and shut my eyes and listen to the music, and the vision of a dancing figure would appear to me, putting all these guys' steps together. I guess in a way that was the Creator helping me. I dance hard, because Wakonda shows me how to do it, and he makes it easy for me.

When a Ponca singer sings, the singing and the music make you dance. That's why I follow those singers around, because of their ability to get into your soul and make you want to dance. Some singers don't move you, but a Ponca singer will move you in your heart and mind — they make it easy to dance longer.

The feathers on Ponca dance bustles are often stripped. This allows them to hang down and flutter in the wind, like the ribbons on our shirts. The bells on this bustle are often used on the skirts of Ponca women (fig. 52). They are widely called "hawk bells."

In the Museum

I am sorry for my Ponca people that there is so little Ponca material in museums. I've been to quite a few museums all over the United States, and I have not seen many things that were Ponca; I was happy to find so much here at the museum. At least we are preserving something for the good of my people.

I don't want to be the only one of my people to look at these Ponca objects. I don't want to go back home and say, "I went to New York City and I got to see all these Ponca things." I would like to be a messenger and a teacher and an educator between the museum and my people. I don't want anyone to think I am knowledgeable about everything, which is not true. I'm learning, just like anybody else.

It's very important to have these things here for our younger generation, for the education of our children, and our grand-children on down. When I go back I'm going to tell them, "If you ever get a chance to go to New York City, you go visit this place and see what our Ponca people have done."

We will never know how the Ponca objects represented here were collected by the museum from my people. They have them, that's the main thing, and now we should respect these objects. We need to understand that the museum is preserving the Ponca materials for us, and trying to educate other museums about the collection. We need to teach other people. That's what I'm going to tell my people when I go back.

Round House and Sacred Circle

All Indian ceremonies are held in a sacred circle — our cycle of life is a sacred circle from infancy to old age. The tipis, mud lodges, and hogans were round; the sacred objects in nature (sun, earth, moon, for example) — and even such natural objects as bird nests — are round. We believe in the sacredness of this hoop of life. This belief is the reason we need a round house.

When the Poncas were first brought down to Indian territory from Niobrara, Nebraska, we had four round houses, where men's and women's societies held their ceremonies. The Hethuska Society had one of these round houses near the Arkansas River. That was where we held our ceremonies. But we haven't had one of these houses for a long time. We would like to have a round house again — with the round house we will be able to regain a little bit of what we had and pass it on to our children and grandchildren.

Through the donations of Hethuska Society members, we purchased 3.75 acres of land at the White Eagle Ponca Reservation from a Ponca tribal member, which means that the land will remain under government trust. On this land, we plan to build a ceremonial round house for the Hethuska Society, so that we will have a permanent house. The round house will be about a hundred feet in diameter, with walls approximately twelve feet high. There will be an entrance facing east, two dressing rooms for the dancers, and restrooms. We will have an outside cook

PONCA DELEGATION IN WASHINGTON, D.C., NOVEMBER 14, 1877.

JACKSON CAT. 1094. (P3413)

FIGURE 53
PONCA BLOUSE.
CLOTH WITH RIBBONWORK, 50.9 X 49.6 CM. (12.839)

shack with a roof and open canvas sides. We will dance twice a year as a society and use the house for other ceremonies — adoptions, namings, funerals, and memorial family feasts, for example.

PERSONAL HISTORY

I was born and raised on the Osage reservation in Gray Horse. I'm related to almost all the Osage in this area and to everybody in the Ponca tribe. I'm half Ponca and half Osage; both tribes are Siouan. I'm looking at work from both groups.

I received good teaching from the descendants of three chiefs — Big Elk, Standing Buffalo, and Big Snake. They would sit and talk to me for hours about Ponca culture and ways. A lot of the things I learned from these people apply to my life today.

On the Osage side, I didn't get as much from my grandpa as I should have. I was awfully young when he passed away. Today, I'm afraid a lot of this knowledge is going to be lost, and my children, my grandchildren, and my great-grandchildren are not going to get the opportunity to learn about these things.

I want non-Indian people to have a better understanding of our culture, beliefs, and religion. All of the objects here are related to our religion in some way, and I think we have to educate the outsiders.

SELECTIONS

This blouse is made from taffeta or silk; Ponca women used calico for everyday wear (fig. 53). If the women were going to town or to visit with their friends, they'd put on their best dresses. Then, just to look pretty, they would use metal sequins, and little metal fringes, when they could get them.

The design of this blouse is one that has been in use for many years. For as long as I can remember, my aunts wore this same sailor-collar design on their blouses. When my wife makes a blouse, she puts a sailor collar on the back.

✖

MAN WITH OSAGE GIRL IN RIBBONWORK BLANKET, CA. 1900. PAUL WARNER COLLECTION. (P17335)

My mother was a bridesmaid at an Osage wedding when I was in elementary school. They gave away a whole corral of horses, and my mother got the first pick. They don't wear these outfits at weddings any more (fig. 54). Now, they wear them in a traditional ceremony in which they "change the drum." This outfit is given to the new drum keeper. You see the women coming down the road with these hats and wedding coats, blankets, and moccasins, but underneath this outfit they have on their own clothing. They take the outfit off right in the arena, and they put it on the new drum keeper. They do this in the sacred circle.

It is a great responsibility to "keep the drum." A new drum keeper is given a drum during a special ceremony. The drum represents the keeper's ongoing obligations to his community. The responsibilities include feeding all the people in the community and ensuring that all the camps have groceries, and

· 132 ·

FIGURE 54
OSAGE WOMAN'S WEDDING OUTFIT (THIS PAGE AND OPPOSITE).
CLOTH, BROADCLOTH, RIBBON, GERMAN SILVER, FEATHER PLUMES, AND BEADS.
MILITARY-STYLE COAT: LENGTH 120.1 CM.; ARROWHEAD SASH: LENGTH 253.6 CM.; HAT: LENGTH 40.7 CM. (23.7300)

FIGURE 54B

OSAGE WEDDING HAT (SEE FACING PAGE).

FIGURE 55

OSAGE GAME STICKS.

BEADED RATTLE MADE WITH TIN CAN; TWO POINTING STICKS WITH CUT FEATHER DECORATION;

TWELVE BEADED COUNTING ARROWS WITH HORSEHAIR TRIM. POINTING STICKS:

LENGTH 50.9 CM.; COUNTING ARROWS: LENGTH 43 CM.; RATTLE: LENGTH 46.5 CM. (23.9267)

wood to burn. The drum is passed periodically from keeper to keeper, so that many people in the community can share these responsibilities, but it must first be accepted by the new drum keeper before it is passed. Some families keep the drum for years, because nobody else will accept the expense involved with being the keeper.

✖

The Osage play a traditional hand game with sticks (fig. 55). The object of the game is to guess who has a small item in their hand. Every time you guess correctly, you get a stick. You must win all six sticks to win the game.

In the old days, the singers sang hand-game songs while the game was played. At the end of each game, they would sing a Round Dance song. All the ladies would get up and put their shawls on and dance to the music. Then they would sit down and sing a giveaway song. They would pass out gourds to people in the audience, who would stand and shake the gourds. After that, people would put a donation up on the table.

They still play hand games today at Gray Horse. I get invitations to come and play. They raise funds with the money gathered at the games. Years ago, the winner would get a pig or horse. Now, the players put money or groceries on each side of the game, and that's what they play for.

ON NATIVE PEOPLES

I think it's important for people to realize that we natives are not really "Indians." It's a good thing Columbus was not looking for Turkey, or we'd be called turkeys. Another thing I think is important is that we are not a tribe. The Bureau of Indian Affairs put that word "tribe" on us — Osage tribe and Ponca tribe. They might have had tribes across the ocean, like the Viking tribes, but Wakonda didn't put us here on Grandmother Earth as tribes, but as big families. We are one great big family. The Sioux have a good term for this — *Mitakuye Oyasin*, meaning "we're all related."

A lot of our tribes don't know their own traditions, teachings, or ways. And it's a shame, because it seems that somebody could have made the effort to preserve some of that for themselves. When I give lectures that's the first thing I say: "You find out where you are and where you came from." Learn about your people, because someday your children and grandchildren will ask what their purpose is on Grandmother Earth, and you're not going to know. It was almost too late for me when I wanted to find out. Almost all our elders were gone by that time.

Get all the books you can find. A lot of these are written by white men, so read lots of different books and make comparisons. Then you can make your own decisions. That's when you've got to go and fast — and sacrifice — and let the spirits help you. And they will help you — but you have to have faith. They'll give you the understanding and wisdom of your people. It's hard to believe what I'm telling you, but I know it's true.

Miguel Puwainchir and **Felipe Tsenkush**, Shuar Indians from the eastern lowlands of Ecuador, have each held leadership positions in the oldest indigenous organization in Ecuador, the *Federación Interprovincial de Centros Shuar-Achuar*, which is dedicated to defending Shuar-Achuar rights.

Puwainchir and Tsenkush are interested in showing the full range of material culture produced by their people, as well as the effects of colonization and missionization on Shuar and Achuar communities. It is of crucial importance to them that their society be regarded as a living culture. During their visit to NMAI, they were also concerned with providing accurate information about objects and informing the outside world about the Shuar and Achuar people.

(*In photo*: Puwainchir, *left*; Tsenkush, *right*)

"History will judge those who have destroyed our culture and our rights. We have to value our culture and the outside world has to respect that cultural right."

MIGUEL PUWAINCHIR AND FELIPE TSENKUSH

· 137 ·

WE ARE A COMMUNITY

We want to show the world that we are an organized people. In the future we don't want to end up engraved in a museum's exhibit. We want our music and dance, our songs to nature, to our jungles, and to our motherland performed by our people themselves while they are alive. We don't want to be thought of as dead people to be exhibited in a museum, described in a book, or recorded on film — that is not our tradition. We are a community like any other community in the world. When we go back to our communities, we will tell them that at the museum we have seen the work of our parents and grandparents who — maybe naively — handed over these sacred objects, which are our people's property, heritage, and patrimony. They handed them over without fully realizing the implications. That is our message, and that is why our participation in this project is so important. We want to share our thoughts, philosophy, and principles as an organization so our fellow indigenous peoples of the Americas and the world will know that we have the capacity to get organized and defend ourselves. The industrialized world wants to destroy our land and contaminate the atmosphere in which we live, which will kill our people and many others. Today, the entire world should be worried about protecting the few remaining Amazonian forests. That is why we got organized — we know that we have to be organized in order to survive and defend our rights. Nobody will save us but our own people.

WOMEN'S THINGS

Male and female objects should not be stored or exhibited together. Among the female objects is this stone piece, a talisman for good crops (fig. 56). Called *nantar* and stored in a ceramic vessel, it is then buried in the middle of the family's garden. A song called *anent* is sung to the stone to maintain the presence of Nunkui, the goddess of the garden. This particular stone is used to bring success in growing yucca or manioc. Today, the missionaries are trying to tell our people that our goddess Nunkui is the Virgin Mary, and that we should sing to Mary and worship representations of her. These missionaries are trying to impose themselves on us and create total confusion. We do not accept this.

✖

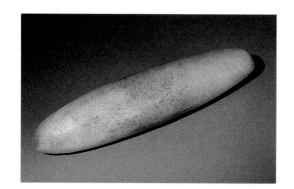

FIGURE 56
SHUAR OR ACHUAR *NANTAR* (TALISMAN).
QUARTZITE, LENGTH 14.5 CM. (1.1775)

SHUAR FAMILY. RÍO UPANO, ECUADOR, 1935.

(P15365)

SHUAR OR ACHUAR WOMEN PREPARING *CHICHA*, 1935.

ORIENTE, ECUADOR. (P12648)

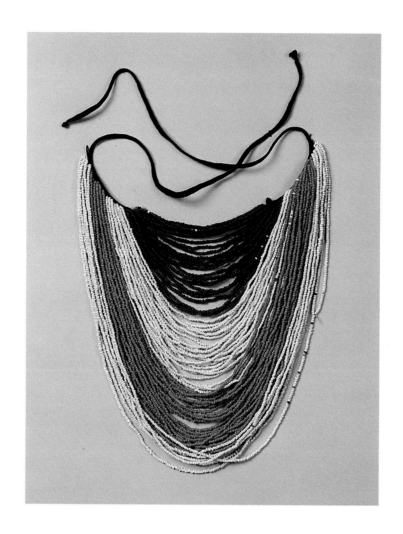

FIGURE 57
SHUAR OR ACHUAR *NUNKUTAI* (WOMAN'S BEAD NECKLACE).
67.5 X 21.5 CM. (18.8770)

This bead necklace, called *nunkutai/shauk jeamu*, is worn by women only for dances and special occasions (fig. 57). The beads or *shauk* are not artificial European glass beads, but natural beads. There is a story about the origin of these beads, which are believed to come from a lake. A Shuar man committed adultery and fled to an uninhabited part of the forest with his lover. They lived there for a long time and had children. During this time he discovered the source of the natural beads in a lake. This lake was guarded by carnivorous birds, snakes, and other animals, and in order to collect the beads, the man had to bring meat to the lake for them to eat. One day he decided to return to his village to trade the beads. But the family of the woman with whom he had committed adultery killed him and his whole family. So now, nobody knows the source of these natural beads.

Another type of nunkutai is made with natural and artificial beads and cricket bones strung on cotton fiber. The metal beads (*sarsea*) were introduced to the Shuar and Achuar by Catholic priests because they resemble rosary beads. The missionaries brought rosary beads with them to teach the Indians how to pray, and the Shuar and Achuar liked to wear the beads as ornaments. This type of necklace, therefore, is an example of the initial contact between the priests and the Shuar and Achuar and the Indians' acculturation into Catholic life.

✖

Chicha is a fermented beverage made from masticated yucca. Bowls called *amamuk* are used to serve the drink to the head of the household and to special guests (fig. 58). Chicha bowls generally have protruding bases, pretty designs, and polished surfaces. The protruding base makes the bowl easier to hold. Women make all the pottery and each family has its own designs. A wooden stick, called *taink*, is used by women to mash the yucca for the preparation of chicha.

✖

A belt or *shakap* is worn by women for dances and special rituals. It is made of a woven cotton band decorated with hanging strands of artificial and natural beads and pieces of cut shell. The shell comes from a land snail called *kunku*, which the Shuar do not eat.

FIGURE 58
SHUAR OR ACHUAR *AMAMUK* (BOWL).
PAINTED BUFF GLAZED WARE, 8 X 20.5 CM. DIAM. (19.4759)

MEN'S THINGS

Impermeable baskets or *pitiak* are used by men, who make all the baskets, to carry delicate and sacred objects over long distances. This basket is tightly woven with two layers of a fiber called *káap* and a layer of palm leaves in between from either the *achu* or *pumpú* tree (fig. 59). The lining of leaves makes the basket waterproof. While there are other similar baskets in the collection, this one is the most finely woven, so it was probably made for someone's personal use and not for sale. The handles on the cover were designed for use with a carrying strap, which is generally made of *yunkua,* a softer fiber that can be tied around the head or shoulders. These baskets are still made and used today.

✖

This quiver is called *tunta* and is used by men for hunting (fig. 60). It holds darts that are used with a blowgun (*uum*) to hunt monkeys and birds. The gourd container or *tsapa* contains natural cotton fibers of the ceibo tree. Ceibo fibers are wrapped around the darts to help them fly. The strip of palm wood that is wrapped around the gourd is used to clean the blowgun. The

FIGURE 59
SHUAR OR ACHUAR *PITIAK*
(IMPERMEABLE CARRYING BASKET).
VEGETAL FIBERS, PALM LEAVES, AND *AWACHA* FEATHERS,
305 X 27.5 CM. DIAM. (20.351 (TOP); 20.358 (BOTTOM))

FIGURE 60
SHUAR OR ACHUAR *TUNTA* (QUIVER FOR BLOWGUN DARTS).
BAMBOO AND GOURD, LENGTH 63 CM. (20.379)

tips of the darts are dipped in poison and the piranha jaw is used to cut a groove near the point so that the tips break off inside the animal. *Uyunt* are monkey-fur bags that identify a man as a successful hunter. The skin used to make the bag comes from a monkey that the hunter has killed. The Shuar and Achuar call these monkeys *washi* or *yakum.*

✖

This feathered crown is called *tawasap* in Shuar (fig. 61). It is worn as a symbol of bravery and authority by older men and political leaders during celebrations and other special occasions. The crown consists of a woven cotton band, red and yellow toucan or *tsukanka* feathers, and black feathers of a bird called *awacha.* The danglers, which resemble earrings, are made of toucan feathers and human hair. Human hair, generally from men, is taken only from living people when they cut their hair.

MEN'S AND WOMEN'S THINGS

Both men and women use red pigment to paint their faces and bodies and to decorate a variety of objects, especially pottery. The nut used to make the

FIGURE 61
SHUAR OR ACHUAR *TAWASAP* OR *ETZENGRUTAY* (MAN'S HEADBAND).
TOUCAN FEATHERS, LENGTH 114.5 CM. (18.9111)

FIGURE 62
SHUAR OR ACHUAR *AKITIAI* (EAR OR SIDEBURN ORNAMENTS).
BEETLEWING COVERS AND TOUCAN FEATHERS, LENGTH 29 CM. (8.4234)

container for this pigment is called *sua*, the container is called *karit*, and the red paint is called *ipiak,* or *achiote* in Spanish.

These earrings or sideburn ornaments, called *akitiai/tirinsanam nenatai*, may be worn by men or women (fig. 62). They are made of beetlewing covers and are decorated with toucan feathers. In Shuar, the beetle is called *wauwau*.

✖

A hair comb called *temash* is made by men — because they are the weavers — but used by both men and women (fig. 63). The comb is made out of a palm wood called *iniayua kunkuk'* or *pintiu* and the design is woven with cotton threads. These combs are still being made today.

✖

Medallions of the Virgin were used by the Salesian (Catholic) missionaries to conquer, evangelize, and "civilize" the Shuar and Achuar peoples. We want to show how Western colonization succeeded in devaluing what was ours and imposing cultural values that were foreign to us. The missionaries used medallions of the Virgin to illustrate who they thought would save us. When this supposedly superior culture arrived, the Shuar and Achuar became an "inferior" culture. The destructive processes of colonization and evangelization are represented in this and many other objects. History will judge those who have destroyed our culture and our rights. We have to value our culture and the outside world has to respect that cultural right.

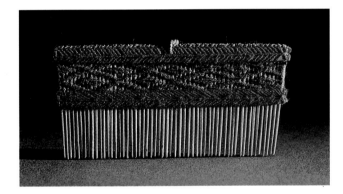

FIGURE 63
SHUAR OR ACHUAR *TEMASH* (COMB).
PALM WOOD WOVEN WITH COTTON THREADS, LENGTH 7 CM. (20.435)

Bonifacia Quispe Fernandez and **Tomás Huanca Laura** are both Aymara (*Qulla*, as they refer to themselves) from the La Paz region of Bolivia. An accomplished weaver, Fernandez heads the *Centro de Madres*, an organization involved in collective work projects of village women. Huanca, an anthropologist and professor at the University of La Paz, has written extensively on Aymara culture. He is a contributor to NMAI's *Native American Dance: Ceremonies and Social Traditions* (1992).

In their tour of the NMAI collection, Huanca and Fernandez focused their attention on works that are quintessentially Aymara in either their religious significance or everyday utility. Both deeply involved in the long, proud history of the Aymara people, they are equally devoted to maintaining their cultural traditions — often in the face of the erosive influence of contemporary urban life.

"Our ancestors are still present and alive. Returning back home we can weave exactly the same textiles as we see in the museum. These things are not that hard to do."

BONIFACIA QUISPE FERNANDEZ AND TOMÁS HUANCA LAURA

· 147 ·

AYMARA WOMAN WEAVING PONCHO, 1927.
BOLIVIA. PHOTO BY A.H. VERRILL. (P9138)

THE INKAS

Most of the Aymara today believe that the Inka were the most powerful people in their time, but not in a bad sense. It wasn't like colonialism. They did enforce tribute, but the Inka also taught the people things. They traded and exchanged goods. The relationship went in both directions.

Aymara today think of the Inka as being godlike. The Inka are still looking over the people – they're still alive and some day they'll come back. The Inka spoke Quechua, although some people might say they spoke Aymara first.

Tiwanaku is the name of an ancient urban center located near the southern shore of Lake Titicaca in Bolivia. The people who inhabited Tiwanaku are considered the ancestors of the Aymara. Tiwanaku grew from a small agricultural community around A.D. 100 to become the religious center of a large empire before it was abandoned around A.D. 1200. The Aymara communities remained in the same place – the highlands – after the collapse of Tiwanaku. The Inkas, who came around 1425, are of the valley region and have myths of origin in *Isla del Sol* (Sun Island). Sun Island in Lake Titicaca is the legendary birthplace of Manco Capac, the first Inka, who is said to have founded the Inka dynasty. The Inkas thought that they were descendants of the Tiwanaku, making them "the royal family."

Some Aymara artifacts show the Inka presence. The *q'iru* (cup) shape, for example, was developed in Tiwanaku times and later adopted by the Inka. This q'iru (fig. 64) could be very important because it represents the two cultures: the Tiwanaku and the Inka. The central band of the q'iru represents one of the main symbols of Tiwanaku – the sacred staircase. This staircase symbolizes the

FIGURE 64
INKA *Q'IRU* (CUP).
WOOD WITH PAINTED REPRESENTATIONS OF HUMAN AND GEOMETRICAL FIGURES,
HEIGHT 19.7 CM. (6.5838)

heavens, earth, and the underground. On the upper section, we see an Inka man with all his symbols of royalty and authority: his staff, shield, and headdress. The q'iru is not Tiwanakan, however; the Inka adopted the symbol of the sacred staircase.

THREATENED TRADITIONS

Young women today tend to forget about traditional weavings. It's easy to buy clothes that come from the factories because such clothing is very cheap and colorful.

Many of these young women work in the city as servants or domestic workers and do not want to be identified as Indians. There is a lot of discrimination against rural people in the city.

One does not see the older type of weavings anymore, the ones with the combination of colors and large stripes. The modern young native generation is not interested anymore; they do not give any importance to those olden objects. The new garments done by machine are the favorites among the youth. Since they often work in cities, the young people really do not pay any attention or attach much importance to handmade weavings. Even when they work in trading and in related businesses, the young ladies buy more of the machine-made clothes of non-traditional fabric. That is the reason why this kind of handmade clothing is disappearing: people are ashamed to wear it in the cities.

Other traditional objects are also falling out of use. The *chhaxraña*, a comb made from a tree similar to a big cactus, is not as practical for carrying as a modern machine-made comb, and that is why people do not use it anymore (fig. 65). Besides, this kind of olden comb pulls a bit on your hair: another reason for people not using it. But there are still old-fashioned ladies with these ancient combs. It's just the younger ones who prefer the modern plastic ones.

Today's q'iru are made from metal, like silver or copper. We can't make this kind of cup from wood anymore — the wooden q'iru is just for ceremonial offerings (fig. 66).

Similarly, certain kinds of pottery are not being made much these days. Or the people make

FIGURE 65
INKA *CHHAXRAÑA* (COMB).
WOOD AND WOOL, 7.6 X 4.5 CM. (16.9805)

things just for tourists. There are communities still specializing in making some of this kind of traditional pottery, but they sell it to other communities. Or sometimes, in seasonal markets, communities exchange pottery for other items, such as animals and frozen dried potatoes. Because of the availability of plastic and metal from the outside world, however, the connection between many traditional objects and the community system is being lost.

Yet our ancestors are still present and alive. Returning back home we can weave exactly the same textiles as we see in the museum. These things are not that hard to do.

CENTRO DE MADRES/ SUKA QULLU

In our communities the women are organized. We have, for example, been organizing a mothers' center in our community. In addition, the women work with *Suka Qullu*, an organization set up to promote the ancient Tiwanaku technique of planting potatoes. From Suka Qullu an individual borrows money. With that money we rent land in order to plant potatoes in coordination with *Centro de Madres*. We also work on knitting sweaters and other items,

FIGURE 66

TIWANAKU OR INKA *Q'IRU* (CUP).

PAINTED AND INCISED WOOD, HEIGHT 15.2 CM. (13.6900)

and we weave clothes, coordinating our work with the Suka Qullu organization.

Whatever we produce in our center, we sell in the city of La Paz, though some of our center's woven goods — such as *tari* (small cloths used to carry food to the fields, among other uses) — are sold in the center itself. Work like this sells quickly, because other weavers do not make these ancient styles anymore and there is a demand for handmade woven goods.

TARI

At home we make tari, of which there are two types: *Mirint*, for everyday use, and *Istalla*, used for special occasions, such as a marriage ceremony (that one is white).

In our everyday sheepherding, we carry our *ququ* (lunch) in a tari made from ordinary sheep wool, and for special occasions, such as a party or potato planting, we use a nice tari made from llama wool (fig. 67). The tari are made one whole piece at a time. There are ornaments, such as fringes, that are no longer done today. Some ornaments involve combining colors into a rainbow pattern. Nowadays, large wide stripes are woven into the design; in olden times weavings were done with many small stripes. The larger striped tari are woven for use in important activities, such as planting and other ceremonies.

A *phullu* is a wide rectangular woman's shawl. A *qarwa phullu* (llama shawl) is used by appointed dignitaries, such as the traditional authorities (the mayor, for example, or the mayor's wife). They are the ones with the right to use these textiles.

Women use *ch'uspita* (one little bag) to carry money (fig. 68). We keep it tied up with a blended color thread called *ch'ankha*. We tie it up with the idea of keeping the money in and attracting money to it. The ch'ankha has to be llama wool, because sheep wool does not attract money or fortune. Llama always attracts fortune and money.

· 152 ·

FIGURE 67
AYMARA *TARI* (BLANKET), USED AS CARRYING CLOTH
FOR BABIES OR BURDENS.
LLAMA WOOL, 86.4 X 81.3 CM. (5.9555)

FIGURE 68
AYMARA *CH'USPITA* — "ONE LITTLE BAG" (KNITTED BAG).
WOOL, 24.1 X 14 CM. (21.7385)

TRADITIONAL AND RITUAL CLOTHING

Every occasion has its own style of clothing. A *wak'a* (waistband) is for a baby — it is a baby wrapper. In the highland communities, parents wrap their babies with many kinds of clothing in the belief that this practice will help prevent physical deformations of the hands, feet, spinal cord, and so on. They believe that by wrapping the baby's hands, feet, and whole body, the baby will grow straight, the bones will not be crooked. On farms in the highlands, babies wrapped with these clothes are carried on their mothers' backs. Babies will be wrapped like this until they are four to five months old.

Among the Aymara women, single women dress fancier and more neatly than married women. Married women are not that careful in their dress. Married women wear mostly dark clothes, while single, available girls dress up in light and colorful dresses. You do not touch the hands of single women even in dancing — you use handkerchiefs. But the married women touch each others' hands.

FIGURE 69
AYMARA LLAMA FIGURINE.
SILVER, HEIGHT 5.3 CM. (22.1901)

COLLAS MUSICIANS, 1927. BOLIVIA. PHOTO BY A.H. VERRILL. (P9140)

SOME SPECIAL CEREMONIES

Wari Katuya is a very important hunting ceremony that takes place before the harvest begins. During the ceremony, a young man is selected to impersonate a *wari* (vicuña, an animal related to the llama). A *wiska* (wool rope) made from llama is tied around his neck. Then he runs away, up into the mountains. Thirty or forty people chase after him, pretending that they are hunting a vicuña. Capturing him, which is very difficult, is like capturing a real vicuña. Once captured, he is ceremonially butchered, and meat, represented by slices of pear, is distributed among the people. They say the "meat" is fresh vicuña meat. Meanwhile, the women dance and sing vicuña and fox songs. These are pretty songs. After everyone comes down from the mountains, they go to someone's home in order to share a real meal. The sponsors of Katuya provide the potatoes and meat. Vicuña blood is sprinkled on the earth as an offering to Pachamama (Mother Earth), the special part of the meat is given to the authorities and the elders, and the rest is shared by the whole community.

The *q'urawa* (rope for throwing stone) is used for a ceremonial event at Christmas. This colored rope is not for sheepherding. The q'urawa used for sheepherding is not colored, but made from black and white natural-color wool. Colored ropes are used for selecting authorities who will be charged with leading the community in every aspect of life, according to the ancient tradition of our ancestors. The q'urawa are placed on the table with pear fruits. There are four persons around the table — the other people there are the audience. Once the godfather and godmother are selected, they receive the q'urawa as a sign of authority. They settle grievances and problems among individuals and communities, like a shepherd who takes care of his flock. In this ceremony they use q'urawa for throwing stones, represented by pears, to the surrounding people. Whoever is hit has to settle his accounts with the authorities.

Qarwa sullu (llama fetus) is used when praying to Pachamama. Others, for example *khuchi sullu* (pig fetus), can be used if a person is very sick. The native priest could use this fetus in a case of sickness to exchange illness; the fetus would represent the ill person. Once the sacrifice is offered, it is buried in the ground. Every spirit protector prefers a different type of animal — it could be llama fetus, sheep fetus, pig fetus, and so on. Spirits such as mountains and Mother Earth prefer llama fetus because they are beneficent spirits. When this offering is made, the fetus is not alone. It goes combined with special candies, flowers, dry fruits, sugar, *q'uwa* (a native aromatic plant) and other herbs, white llama wool, birds, and coca leaf. These offerings are celebrated by a native high priest — a common person cannot offer these things. If a common person were to do it, his life would be in danger. Native priests are our cultural guardians. They determine what belongs to our culture and what is intrusive, foreign. For example, sheep are not native; therefore, they are not part of our ritual culture. Llama, yes — llama is at the heart of our cultural existence (fig. 69).

Illa, the unseen spirit of Andean domestic animals, is petitioned annually by sprinkling a special winelike liquor upward into the air and down onto the earth. Each family has an Illa at home. The ceremony is done by the head of the family. Little miniature animals are lined up nicely — often llamas, because the family is Aymara and wishes for more wealth, abundance, in llamas.

In the mining caves, the miners believe that there is a spirit called *Tiyu-achachila* (guardian of the mines). In order to extract minerals, you have to offer some coca leaves, liquor, cigarettes, asking the spirit to keep the miners well, prevent accidents, and allow the extraction of minerals.

Manuel Ríos Morales (Zapotec from the Northern Sierras of Oaxaca) is a social science teacher in Oaxaca, Mexico. He is currently an associate professor-researcher at the *Centro de Investigaciónes y Estudios Superiores en Antropología Social* (Center for Research and Higher Studies in Social Anthropology). Ríos has also been a rural teacher in various indigenous communities, and has conducted research relating to the Mixtecos, Tlapanecas, and Nahuas in the state of Guerrero, Mexico. As part of the Zapotec community of Zoogocho, he plays the clarinet in the community's band.

Ríos is interested in pointing out that despite the fragmentation and cultural diversity among the various subgroups of the Zapotecs, a shared unity — based on their material, ritual, and symbolic culture — can be observed among them and with other groups in Mexico. His encounter with the museum's collection revolved around the ways in which ethnic identity manifests itself in communities through religious ceremonies, rituals, music, dance, and specific clothing.

"We Zapotecs are not the same people as we once were, but we still preserve our beliefs. We still have many needs, as well as some conveniences that have helped and changed us. But we continue to preserve a communal identity based upon our language and music, and upon our traditions and culture."

MANUEL RÍOS MORALES

· 157 ·

The Zapotec People

There are about 450,000 speakers of the Zapotec language in Oaxaca, making the Zapotecs the largest ethnic group in the state. They can be subdivided into four important and distinct subgroups: the Zapotecs of the Valley in central Oaxaca; the Zapotecs of the Isthmus in the Tehuantepec region; the Zapotecs of the Southern Sierras; and finally the Zapotecs of the Northern Sierras.

We Zapotecs are not the same people as we once were, but we still preserve our beliefs. We still have many needs, as well as some conveniences that have helped and changed us. But we continue to preserve a communal identity based upon our language and music, and upon our traditions and culture.

Part of Our Own History

Much has been written about us from the perspective of the outsider, but our own story – written by our own people with an inside perspective – remains to be told.

It is important for indigenous people to know that there are objects from our own cultures outside of our communities, as is the case with the museum's collections. These objects need to be studied, but not for the purpose of separating what is Zapotec from Mixtec. While it is important to determine the provenance of each piece, it is more important to recognize the relationship among the many American Indian cultures. Our interest is to feel acknowledged in the symbolic and material expressions of each object, and to learn what these objects tell us about our past, our history, our communities, and our identity.

A careful study of the many archaeological pieces from Oaxaca in the museum could demonstrate the cultural continuity between the past and present in the Valley, the Sierras, and the Isthmus. A better understanding of the complexity of the Zapotec culture could also be achieved. As a way of enabling us to reconstruct our history, these objects therefore have enormous significance for all indigenous communities.

The diversity of the objects in the museum's collection encompasses more than a single culture, territory, or geographic region. For example, according to the museum's records, this fragment of a mosaic mask is Mixtec, and was discovered in the District of Acatlán, State of Puebla (fig. 70). The Mixtecs not only lived in Oaxaca, but also in the present states of Puebla and Guerrero. This Mixtec piece, therefore, expresses a social identity that extends beyond administrative, political, or regional frontiers; it reflects the history of the migrant Mixtecs scattered throughout various parts of Mexico, and of Mexican populations situated today in Tijuana, Mexico, and Los Angeles, California.

In pre-colonial times, many areas and settlements were shared. In the Valley of Oaxaca for example, Monte Albán was occupied by Zapotecs and Mixtecs, and sometimes it is difficult to determine exactly what elements belonged to each culture. What is more important for us, however, is that we acknowledge our common history and culture.

Fiestas

In the daily life of our communities there is a sacred space reserved for the reaffirmation of our beliefs and identity through rituals,

FIGURE 70
MIXTEC MASK (IN TWO PIECES).
WOOD INLAID WITH TURQUOISE, LENGTH 17 CM. (10.8712)

FIGURE 71
ZAPOTEC MASK.
CARVED AND PAINTED WOOD, DIAM. 30.5 CM. (20.1635)

celebrations, music, and dance. These festivities generally take place at specific times and places.

Fiestas constitute the culmination of the whole process of production and reproduction, of ritual and legend, that is intimately related to the thoughts, beliefs, and ways of being of our communities. Each fiesta coincides with a pre-Hispanic tradition that is related to the cycles of life and agricultural production. At present, these events are also celebrated with a representation of the patron saint of the community. In the same way that each Zapotec house has a sacred space that serves as an altar, every town has a church or chapel where communal ceremonies are held. It is also common for the name of a town to be the same as the name of its patron saint — for example, San Andrés Solaga, San Bartolomé Zoogocho, San Francisco Cajonos, and Santa María Tavehua.

DANCES

Among indigenous groups, dances, together with music, constitute symbolic spaces of a group's identity. It is within this context that the diverse expressions of dance must be analyzed and understood. Each society or group constructs its particular identity based upon its own history, context, beliefs, knowledge, and perceptions. For the Zapotecs, this process is also seen in the diversity of their dances, which reflect their experiences, lifestyles, situations, differences, and fears. The purpose of these dances is also to give thanks to the gods, while at the same time providing entertainment to the audience. The various dances include references to animals (tigers, mosquitos, turkeys, rats); events (Conquest, Santiago, Malinche, Huenches, San Marcos); other ethnic groups (Negritos, Mixes, Tehuanos, Aztecas, Zotas); and humor (Revueltos, Cuerudos, Sombrerotes, Minifaldas).

The dances (*weyhaa'* in Zapotec) are normally danced by eight to sixteen couples accompanied by bands of fifteen to thirty-five wind instruments playing special *sones* for each dance. A *son* is a short one- to two-part melody that is rooted in the style of the colonial period. Each *son* is created specifically for each type of dance. Some dances are accompanied by a double-reed

instrument called a *chirimía* and a small wooden drum made out of a tree trunk. Unlike the other dances, the one called Huenche Nene is accompanied by a small baby, usually represented by a doll, which plays a principal part in the presentation.

Each dance starts with a short introduction called the *registro*, which is repeated at the beginning or end of each *son* or musical piece. Each dance has an average of twelve *sones* that are danced for approximately three or four hours, with rest breaks after every three or four *sones*.

MASKS

Masks are a necessary complement to most dances. The use of masks, an intrinsic part of the dances, is determined by the ceremonial nature of the celebration. The characteristics of each dance determine the particular masks used as well as the costumes that must be worn. The masks, costumes, and dances are not themselves sacred; together within a ceremonial context, however, they are the medium to the sacred. The majority of the Zapotec masks at NMAI come from Yalálag, a representative Zapotec community in the Northern Sierras, where many craftsmen preserve the tradition of mask-making.

Zapotec masks are different from those of other regions because they are made specifically for each dance. The maskmaker usually begins with the forehead and makes small openings at the side or center of the carved eyes to enable the wearer to see. Masks never have hair or ears. Because of its features, this mask can be worn either for the Mixes' or the Huenches Viejos' dance (fig. 71). Unfortunately, the museum's records do not provide additional information about the piece. Many of the masks are made out of *zompancle* and *fresno*, or other woods that are durable as well as easy to carve.

One of the most representative dances of the Northern Sierra region of Oaxaca is the Dance of the Negritos. Since this area does not have a black population, the idea must have been to represent this ethnic group through a dance. The Negrito Dance is characterized by the richness and gracefulness of its choreography and costumes. The elegant costumes are made out of black velvet, decorated with sequins and fringes, and brightly

FIGURE 72
ZAPOTEC URN.
CARVED BLACKWARE, HEIGHT 38.5 CM. (16.6080)

colored ribbons that hang down the back. The mask has two incisors or fangs, and the hat has a toucan beak on the top. All of these characteristics make the performance of this dance a show of mastery, regional music, and great ceremony.

SOME SELECTIONS

According to the museum's records, this ceramic figure comes from the town of Choapan, in a Zapotec region of the Northern Sierras (fig. 72). The Zapotecs in Choapan are a small sub-group who live in the most northerly part of Oaxaca, where it borders Veracruz. Their language is a variation of Zapotec called *Serrano* (from the Sierra). Because very little research has been conducted in this region, it is almost certain that no Zapotec from Choapan knows that the museum owns a piece from this community. This situation lends the piece importance.

✕

The form and craftsmanship of this copper plaque, featuring a human figure wearing an elaborate headdress, clearly correspond to the pre-Columbian Mixtec-Zapotec culture (fig. 73). Without more data, however,

ZAPOTEC WOMAN, 1939. YALÁLAG.
OAXACA, MEXICO. (N37191)
"HERE IS A PICTURE OF A WOMAN FROM YALÁLAG WHOSE HEADDRESS IS JUST LIKE THE ONE DEPICTED ON THE CERAMIC URN IDENTIFIED AS BEING FROM CHOAPAN (SEE FIG. 72). THIS HEADDRESS, PART OF A YALÁLAG WOMAN'S DRESS, SHOWS THE CLOTHING, CULTURE, AND TRADITIONS OF THE ZAPOTEC OF THE NORTHERN SIERRA. YALÁLAG IS ONLY ONE COMMUNITY, BUT IT IS VERY REPRESENTATIVE OF ZAPOTEC CULTURE." —MRM

it is difficult to determine its use and significance among these people.

✖

Among the Mixtecs, more than among the Zapotecs, genealogies, dates, and events were recorded by means of codices (pictorial manuscripts), of which this jade plaque is an example (fig. 74). Deciphering its function and significance is a job for specialists capable of explaining, among other things, who might be represented here and determining the time period for the style of eyes, feet, and hands.

✖

Although there are other objects identified as Zapotec from Oaxaca, the material and form are different from some of the other artifacts that have been found and analyzed from Zapotec sites such as Mitla, Monte Albán, Choapan, and San Pablo Huilá.

FIGURE 73
MIXTEC-ZAPOTEC PLAQUE.
CAST COPPER, LENGTH 8.9 CM. (24.2724)

FIGURE 74
MIXTEC-ZAPOTEC PLAQUE.
CARVED JADE, 15.2 X 8.5 CM. (1.2548)

This ceramic urn from San Pablo Huilá, in the Valley of Oaxaca, is a beautiful and excellent representation of pre-Hispanic Zapotec culture and thought (fig. 75). The piece also reflects the religious and ceremonial nature of Zapotec life today. San Pablo Huilá continues to be an important ceremonial center where Zapotec people from the Valley and the Sierras come together for annual celebrations.

Zaachila, also located in the valley of Oaxaca, was the capital of the Zapotec empire and the residential home of the Zapotec rulers during the pre-Hispanic period. Zaachila represented an entire Zapotec dynasty. The splendor of Zapotec culture was manifested in the palaces, the ornamentation used by kings, and the craftsmanship of ceramic urns and other objects of a sacred nature that were taken from the tombs in which they were originally found.

FIGURE 75
ZAPOTEC URN.
CARVED BLACKWARE, HEIGHT 73.6 CM. (16.4077)

Alejandro Flores Huatta and his niece **Paula Quispe Cruz** (Quechua) are weavers from the island of Taquile, on the Peruvian side of Lake Titicaca. Besides being weavers, Huatta is a musician and Cruz a dancer.

They share an interest in early Quechua and Aymara materials, especially textiles. In their exploration of the NMAI collection, they were particularly motivated by their desire to explore the significance of early iconography in order to relearn and recover lost traditional weaving patterns and techniques.

"People from Taquile do not leave the community to find work. Most people are very shy and it is difficult for them to leave the island and go to other places. Outsiders do not come into the community to live, because we have no donkeys, trucks, or horses. It is hard to move around Taquile's terrain and altitudes. We do everything ourselves — we carry our own burdens up the hills. That is difficult for others, but we are used to it and for us it is very easy."

ALEJANDRO FLORES HUATTA AND PAULA QUISPE CRUZ

· 167 ·

THE LAND

There are more people in Taquile today and there is not enough land. Land is owned by families and passed down from parents to children, and each person within the family has a parcel of land.

We all have our own land; every person has a parcel, and no one can usurp. People from the outside cannot come into Taquile and buy land. If somebody from the community sells their land, then the community takes it back. It can't be sold to outsiders, and this protects us.

If somebody has a little more land than he can use, he must donate it to the community. We request the land, and when the owner agrees, we give him something in return. He must agree to the arrangement.

In the Andes, the climate is very harsh, so people often own small sections of land over a large area. This allows them to grow crops in many different locations, so if there is bad weather at one site, they still have resources in another area. The agricultural land in Taquile is terraced; there are no open fields. The terraces are planted using a sequence of crop rotation, to allow the land to rest between various crops.

We plant potatoes, corn, beans, oca, barley — the crops change with the seasons. There is also a fishing season, and during this time, we till the land and plant the seeds. A family usually also has about twenty-five or thirty sheep. To obtain items such as kerosene and matches, we sell seeds from our crops. This only began recently; before, we traded for all our needs in a bartering system. Now, sometimes people sell traditional arts for cash to buy certain things that are not available through trade.

HOW WE LIVE

Today we are promoting tourism. We have a large cooperative for this purpose. There is a community law, however, that states that there are only certain days when tourists can visit Taquile, and a limited number of tourists can enter the community per day. If too many tourists come, we cannot allow it, because the community may change. We are conscientious about preserving our culture.

When buildings are required for community use, such as schools, churches, or any kind of government building, the community asks someone with extra land to donate the required land. The landowners do this willingly. In Taquile we have churches, a high school and an elementary school, a community center, a post office, and other government buildings. We have almost everything.

People from Taquile do not leave the community to find work. Most people are very shy and it is difficult for them to leave the island and go to other places. Outsiders do not come into the community to live, because we have no donkeys, trucks, or horses. It is hard to move around Taquile's terrain and altitudes. We do everything ourselves — we carry our own burdens up the hills. That is difficult for others, but we are used to it and for us it is very easy.

WEAVING

There are many weavers in Taquile. But not all weavers weave with the same skill. The finest weavers and weaving families are well known throughout the community. Each individual in Taquile wears the clothing identified with his or her own family.

AYMARA GROUP IN TRADITIONAL DRESS, 1929.

BOLIVIA. (29558)

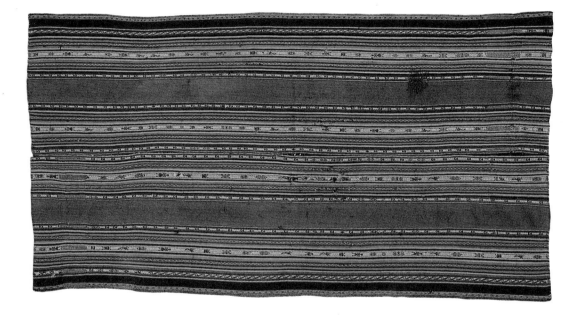

FIGURE 76
QUECHUA *UNKUÑA* (CEREMONIAL TABLECLOTH).
WOOL, 47 X 89 CM. (14.4640)

Women learn how to weave from their mothers and grand-mothers. They start weaving when they are very young, watching the women and learning little by little. For instance, a six- or seven-year-old girl starts by weaving a narrow band, and when she becomes more experienced, she goes on to a wider band, and so on.

As soon as a young woman learns the essentials of each design, she takes off and does her own work, eventually without supervision. All women must learn to weave before they are married; it is a requirement.

One important thing about weaving is that much of the terminology used is Aymara in origin. Even Quechua speakers use Aymara terminology when weaving. Some of the words originated in languages that have since been lost, languages that are even older than Aymara.

SELECTIONS

This textile is called *unkuña* (fig. 76). It is a very old piece, and very special. This unkuña has been used in ceremonies for many years. It is like a ceremonial tablecloth for the altar on which ritual offerings are placed — such as fermented beverages (*chicha*) and coca leaves.

To make this green pigment, we use a plant called *chilca*, and *yana kolpa*, a dark soil. We pick the leaves, cut them with a machete, weigh them, and put them in boiling water. Then we put the wool in and heat it a little more. After that, we remove the wool and add the yana kolpa. We return the wool to the water and boil it for another hour to obtain this shade of green.

One of the designs in this textile is the symbol representing the *katekate* bird. This bird appears in flight with its mouth open. When the katekate flies at sunset, it means that a relative is going to die or something is going to happen to us. But when it flies at dawn, it means good luck. The design of the border, called *sillana*, is like the waves of the sea. The little design with the "X" is called *bandera* (flag). It preserves the memory of Tupac Amaru, the Indian leader who led a revolution in the late eighteenth century. He was killed by four horses, and the X symbolizes his four pieces.

✗

QUECHUA MAN IN TRADITIONAL DRESS
PLAYING FLUTE.
PERU. (37998)

FIGURE 77
QUECHUA MAN'S WEDDING PONCHO.
WOOL, 143.5 X 170.5 CM. (10.6590)

This is a man's wedding poncho (fig. 77). During my grandfather's time, this poncho was still in use. My godfather had a poncho like this, and he gave me one very similar to this one. This type of poncho must be used, and it may be rented, but not loaned. It is traditionally rented by the godfather for the groom. While everyday ponchos are worn over the head, ceremonial ones such as this are worn folded over the shoulder. This poncho is sacred.

The pigments in this textile are from aniline, a synthetic dye. My grandparents and my great-grandparents dyed wool with *cochinilla* dye from the cochineal insect for a brilliant red color. The cochineal insect lives on a cactus. Collecting these insects is a dangerous business, because the thorns of the cactus are so light that they come off and hover in the air. In the Inka's time, the people who collected the insects became blind from getting these thorns in their eyes. Today we are planting cactus all around Taquile to encourage the propagation of the cochineal insects, so that we may once again use this traditional dye. For now, we purchase cochinilla in Ayacucho, in central Peru.

We use similar wedding ponchos today — with the same designs in gray instead of red — except that the ponchos are now made from a different material. The changes happened gradually over a long period of time; little by little they used more gray and less red, so that today the wedding ponchos are all gray. This type of large poncho takes a long time to weave, and the *pallays* (designs) are difficult. Today, the pallays are a little less intricate, so that the ponchos may be woven more quickly.

✘

During the wedding ceremony, the groom wears the wedding poncho, a special *chalina* (scarf), and a pink *chullu* (wool cap). The bride wears a red ceremonial *manta* (shawl) with many designs, and a black hat decorated with flowers. This hat is used as an everyday hat in other communities, but in Taquile it is used only in wedding ceremonies (fig. 78). *Monteras* (bridal hats) always have flowers on them. There are very few monteras on Taquile Island, so these matrimonial hats are rented in the same way as matrimonial ponchos. During the wedding

· 173 ·

FIGURE 78
QUECHUA WOMAN'S WEDDING HAT.
WOOL WITH EMBROIDERED DESIGNS
AND YARN ROSETTES,
42.5 X 44.75 CM. (24.1854)

FIGURE 79
QUECHUA SKIRT.
ALPACA WOOL, 77.25 X 279.5 CM. (21.7449)

ceremony, the bride's hat is lowered to cover her face. After two days, she may take it off. The hat is worn lowered in this fashion for the bride's protection – it is considered bad luck if she sees a widow or "bad people" during this period. Paula's father still makes this kind of hat by hand. He is one of the few who know how to do embroidery. This particular hat is machine-made.

✖

Skirts like this were passed down in a family (fig. 79). This type of skirt comes from the Lake Titicaca area; the purple color comes from a fruit called *mullaka* that is gathered once a year. Today, there is not enough of the fruit to use as a dye, so cochineal dye is used in its place. Purple is only used for special pieces today, because it is very expensive.

The cross design is called *ch'aska*, which means reflecting star. The "X" is called the Cross of the South. The purple is called *pampa*, and the two white stripes are for luck. The skirt is made entirely out of very fine alpaca wool. Because it was finished with a needle, rather than on a loom, it had to have been made for a special occasion. They took great care not to disfigure the designs.

✖

In ancient times, messengers called *chaski* would run from one point to another, where another messenger would be waiting to relay the message to the next chaski. The chaski used a musical instrument similar to this one that could be heard from as far away as five kilometers (fig. 80). We still use music to let one another know what is happening. For instance, there is a special music for mourning, and another kind for use when drinking chicha.

· 175 ·

FIGURE 80
NAZCA PANPIPES.
CERAMIC, 28.5 X 13.5 CM. (11.2563)

Teofila Palafox Herranz and **Juan Olivares** are Ikood (also called Huave) from San Mateo del Mar on the coast of southern Oaxaca in Mexico. Palafox started a weaving cooperative in her town and has traveled widely, including trips to Russia and Chile, selling the group's weavings. Olivares is a fisherman who has worked with several anthropologists to record the cultural history of his people. Also a storyteller, he has appeared at the Smithsonian's Festival of American Folklife.

Although there is little Ikood material among the museum's collections, Palafox and Olivares were inspired by their visit to the museum to discuss significant elements of their cultural life, which includes the division of men and women into very separate worlds. Both also share an abiding interest in the technology and work of traditional life.

"The activities and behavior of women and men were once precisely defined and governed by Ikood tradition. For instance, in ancient times, it was said that if a woman were to touch a man's belongings, they would be spoiled and the man would have bad luck and be unable to catch any fish. That was the belief people had. But it is different today; the customs have changed."

· 177 ·

TEOFILA PALAFOX HERRANZ AND JUAN OLIVARES

Men and Women

In old times it was said that if a woman touched a man's fishnet, it would not be good for fishing and the man would have bad luck, and he would not have any success as a fisherman. That was the belief that people had. But today it is different; the customs have changed. For example, today there are women who weave men's fishnets.

Ikood laws and customs regarding women and men began to disappear around 1950. Before then, there was little contact with people outside the community, and the old customs remained intact — nothing was lost. Eventually, the fishermen (*pescadores*) went to Chiapas and other parts of Mexico, and saw how other people lived. When they came back to their own towns, they brought new customs with them. They returned wearing such items as shoes and watches.

Traditionally, the men fish and the women prepare the fish and take them to market. Women never fish, and men do not go to market. Only women go to the market.

Men were allowed in the market, but these men were generally considered effeminate or drunken; they may not have had a wife or family, or they might have come from another town or colony. In old times, men simply did not go to market except in special cases. A man elected by the municipality as the market's manager would go to maintain order, but for no other purpose.

There was no need for men to go to the market, because the women would go and then tell their husbands what they heard there. The women listened carefully to the vendors and found out where fish had been caught. They would give this information to their husbands or fathers, and the men would go to that place to fish.

In the old days, women in San Mateo cared for the chickens and the pigs, while men were in charge of the donkey, horse, and cow. Women planted tomatoes, *posote* or chilis, and tended the vegetable garden, while men sometimes planted corn. There were some men who farmed, but not many. Most men spent their time fishing.

The activities and behavior of women and men were once precisely defined and governed by Ikood tradition. For instance, in ancient times, it was said that if a woman were to touch a man's belongings, they would be spoiled and the man would have bad luck and be unable to catch any fish. That was the belief people had. But it is different today; the customs have changed.

Clothing Selections by Teofila Palafox

I learned weaving and embroidery designs from my mother. The traditional design is *la Greca* (the Greek key). When you're working with Greca, you notice right away if you make a mistake. The Greca designs are mathematical — if you miss one thread, the mistake is very obvious in the finished design.

A long time ago, the designs developed from purely geometrical form into more naturalistic images. The more experienced weavers began to experiment, to develop the weaving and change the designs. Little by little they added designs representing animals from our region — the heron, white crane, rabbit, horse, goat, sheep.

Weavers would sometimes copy a design from another woman's blouse, or *huipil*. This type of exact duplication was acceptable, but it was not considered proper to improve on the design, because the original weaver would think you were presumptuous.

This kind of huipil is folded along the top, with just a slit for the neck opening (fig. 81). Only the middle section is embroidered. The purple dye used for the thread comes from a snail found in the ocean — you can always smell the sea in pieces with this dye.

FIGURE 81
IKOOD *HUIPIL* (BLOUSE).
WOVEN COTTON, LENGTH 73.7 CM. (20.1718)

Old women in ancient times did not sell these huipiles. A woman who had a huipil when she was married would save it throughout her life. This custom changed when foreigners wanted to buy the huipiles, and some of the weavers preferred to sell their work. But even today, there are women who keep these huipiles, believing that if you marry with a weaving, you must keep it until death, and when you die, you must wear it to your grave.

✖

This is a quality, fully embroidered huipil, the kind people make for their own use (fig. 82). The embroidery is dense and heavy, indicating fine craftsmanship. The older pieces of embroidery from Oaxaca have more filling, more embroidery — embroidery from the top to the bottom. This style of work takes a long time to complete. A simpler style, with less embroidery and more white cloth showing

FIGURE 82
MIXTEC *HUIPIL* (BLOUSE) AND SKIRT.
HUIPIL: WOVEN, EMBROIDERED COTTON, LENGTH 88.9 CM. (19.6047);
SKIRT: WOVEN, EMBROIDERED COTTON, LENGTH 73 CM. (10.965)

through, is made for sale to tourists. This type of fully embroidered huipil is still made today, but only for those willing to pay a high price for the intricate work it involves.

Traditionally, women wore different styles of skirts, or *enredos*, according to their status — whether they were married or single, old or young. There were also various ways of tying the skirts, and assorted belts you could wear with them.

This skirt, like the huipil with which it is pictured here, also features the Greek key design. Both pieces may have been made by the same person. Mixteca skirts are different; they are like a bag that you step inside, instead of a piece of material that you wrap around your waist. The embroidery on this skirt is finished neatly on both sides of the fabric. Some embroideries have a right side and a wrong side, but the finishing here is well done on both sides.

NAHUA WOMAN WITH CHILDREN, CA. 1900.
MEXICO. PHOTO BY ALES HRDLICKA.
(P5057)

JUAN OLIVARES ON FISHING

My grandparents told me that when the Ikoods first arrived in San Mateo they were farmers. When they realized the richness of resources available from the sea, they abandoned farming and became fishermen. During this time, the Zapotecs began farming land neglected by the Ikoods. Territorial boundaries recorded by the Ikoods long ago were lost during the Mexican Revolution, and today, San Mateo is becoming smaller and smaller — the Zapotecs continue to usurp Ikood land for agricultural purposes, while the Ikoods continue to fish.

I began fishing when I was eight years old. My father taught me; he made a small net for me, about one meter long. You learn how to become a fisherman when you are very young. My two grandsons, who are eight and ten years old, are learning now; they fish with their father. That is the way we learn how to fish.

NAHUA WOMAN, CA. 1900. MEXICO.

PHOTO BY ALES HRDLICKA. (P5067)

A fisherman knows the direction of the wind by listening to the singing of the birds. He studies the movement of the wind and the water, and he is aware of the sea's dangers. He knows when and where to catch all kinds of fish, both freshwater and saltwater, and how to cure and dry each one. A fisherman needs to know all of this before he really knows how to fish.

In every fishing canoe, there is one fisherman, the *natang ndoc* (the chief of the net), who knows more than the others; he knows about everything concerning fishing. He is like a captain. The movement of water and changes in the weather — he has to know about these things. He is able to discern when the weather will be a cause for concern, when and if the clouds and wind will bring rain and danger.

In old times, when a fisherman went out to sea, he often carried a harpoon or stick to ward off danger from crocodiles, alligators, or bad spirits. This harpoon was used only on the open sea; it was not for the lagoons. I have never fished in this way, using a stick for protection, but I have seen my father using a stick to defend himself from alligators and bad spirits.

There was once a belief that if you took money with you when you went fishing, you would have bad luck and find no fish. The ocean would tell you that because you have money, you don't need anything from the sea. A long time ago, I remember my father advising me never to take money when fishing because it would bring me bad luck.

Today, everybody carries money when fishing. They need money for transportation to and from the place where they fish. I always take money with me; I use it to pay for a car to get there and then for a car to return. I keep this money in my bag while I am fishing.

OLD TRADITIONS AND CHANGING TIMES

Not long ago, some people came to San Mateo because they had heard that the Ikoods asked for and received rain by saying prayers. These visitors participated in the procession to the sea in which the people pray for water, rain, shrimp, and fish. Later, they came back to San Mateo to thank the authorities, because they had prayed the same way in their community and it had rained. They brought a truck full of tender corn for the entire municipality as a gesture of gratitude. This was not long ago, but the authorities in San Mateo today no longer believe in the old ways.

PRESERVING TRADITIONAL KNOWLEDGE

In the old days, there were no Western doctors in San Mateo. The Ikood people knew how to take care of themselves based on traditional knowledge. Some of the anthropologists who have visited the community say that it is very important to maintain this knowledge, because even today doctors are not always available and the people need to know how to treat themselves. It is crucial that we restore our knowledge of the native plants, the medicinal herbs from San Mateo, because nobody can teach us how to use those plants. We should know our own medicines.

In San Mateo, the *Instituto Nacional Indigenista* has a program designed to encourage the preservation of traditional plants and traditional methods of healing — to preserve them before they are lost. A group of twenty indigenous doctors practicing traditional medicine meets on a regular basis for this purpose. These efforts have not yet reached the national level, but meetings have been taking place at both regional and state levels. We are very few but our numbers are growing.

Tom Hill (Seneca), Director of the Woodland Indian Museum in Brantford, Ontario, is the author-editor of numerous books, catalogues, essays, and scholarly papers, and producer of several films and videos. He is also the general editor for *Creation's Journey: Native American Identity and Belief*, the NMAI book of masterworks from the collection.

As an Indian and museum professional, Hill brings a sharply honed critical perspective to the significant issues of Native American cultural life. He is especially concerned with the need for museums to confront stereotypes and false expectations in their involvement with indigenous peoples and cultures.

"We have sometimes perpetuated stereotypes of Indians, and that has to change. And changing means looking at ourselves and recognizing that we're like everybody else in this world — we have good guys, we have bad guys. We have a spiritual mantle as well as a sense of humor. Maybe because we tend to idealize it, I think we sometimes look at our cultural past too seriously."

TOM HILL

· 185 ·

BOUNDARIES

I'm not an anthropologist, I have not studied material culture. I'm familiar with the museum's collection and I have certain ideas about it, but I'm primarily interested in ideas, in a museum of ideas. I think that our museums have failed because they have not taken risks, they have not gone beyond the artifacts. I think it's our responsibility — if museums are going to be valid institutions in the present and future — to explore these new boundaries, to push the boundaries a little bit further. I'm not advocating controversy for the sake of controversy, but I think we've got to re-think, reinterpret this work. We have to see it anew. Because, really, it's what's behind the artifact that is of true importance.

THE BIG PICTURE

We can't be so ethnocentric anymore. We can't be those smug Iroquoian people, who did all these great and wonderful things. We can blow our own horns — we have a right to and we should — but we have to look for the bigger picture, now more than ever, and see how we fit in, how we interface.

Any genuine culture — if it is a living, breathing culture — involves evolution and change. And the moment we think that our culture is back in the past, back in that museum case, we're in for it. Because we'll always try to aspire to that item in the museum case. And that's not where our culture is. It's happening here, as we look at this video or participate in other kinds of activities. We've got to be able to take the world views, which in a way began in these cases, and bring everything up to speed, to what's happening now.

One of the elements that I most appreciate about the museum's mission is this interfacing, this interaction that is going on, which will, indeed, make those kinds of connections between past and present. Our job doesn't end, however, once we get the show up and rolling. We're still going to have to play an active, interpretive role.

What we have to do — and it is going to be difficult — is make native people feel comfortable moving through the institutional environment of a museum. A museum can be an alien place, as it sometimes is for groups in my area. Our school systems are encouraging familiarity with museums through school visits. People are beginning to develop a kind of vocabulary about the experience, so they're starting to feel less intimidated. Still, it's a foreign environment. So often museums are created to be temples of culture — I think of the Metropolitan Museum of Art as a good example, or even the old Museum of the American Indian. We build these big museums that say Verdi and Columbus, with gigantic Corinthian pillars and big steps that you walk up, and then we do the displays. They're like treasure chests — "Just look at our booty here, our Iroquoian booty." We've got to get away from the "cabinet of curiosities" approach.

A museum may be a wonderful building, but we have to change the way people experience it. We've got to be more user-friendly, we've got to relate the building to the community, the earth. We've got to talk about ideas, we've got to talk about issues, and we've got to talk about beautiful things too. We've got to talk about humor and about all of the things that make human beings the way they are.

SOPHRONIA THOMPSON (TUSCARORA), 1931 OR 1936.
PHOTO BY J.N.B. HEWITT. NATIONAL ANTHROPOLOGICAL ARCHIVES,
SMITHSONIAN INSTITUTION. (J.N.B.H. ALBUM II, #42)

FIGURE 83
OTTAWA WOMAN'S HAT.
WOVEN SWEETGRASS WITH QUILLED BAND,
30.7 X 7.5 CM. (8.6377)

ADAPTATION

We were having a talk once, and somebody said, "When everything is said and done, we'll probably still be around because we
have been able to adapt very well. We have been able to adjust
and still maintain our integrity." People will argue that developments such as tourist art involve a loss of integrity. But it is a
question of survival. Some objects may change, but the world
view doesn't change. The culture itself is based on some very
basic beliefs. And some of those beliefs are evident even in tourist art. Our ability to adapt can be seen in many objects.

You have to remember that there was a lot of pressure on
Native Americans to be Europeanized. People were encouraged
not to look Indian, and they tried hard with what feeble means
they had to accommodate the pressure from the outside community to adapt. So when you see a piece like this woman's
sweetgrass hat with quilled band, you think that its owner
probably could not afford the nickel it would have cost to buy a
hat in the local general store, so she makes her own (fig. 83).
This is a really beautiful piece. Iroquoian people made straw hats
for both men and women, and sometimes, when they had access
to sweetgrass, they put a little bit around the rim. You can just
see some grandmother going off in this hat. I would think it's
one of her best hats — it's a dress hat, the one you would wear to
market or on a trip to town. She spent considerable time and
effort here. She couldn't be herself, yet she is herself because she
uses materials that she has at hand — sweetgrass and quills. And
she decorates it with all the colors that she has — she probably
has dresses these colors, and the hat highlights the dresses
she wears.

· 189 ·

IROQUOIS SILVERSMITH AT WORK.
GRAND RIVER RESERVE, ONTARIO, CANADA.
(P616)

FIGURE 84
HURON ORNAMENTS (BROOCH, PAIR OF BRACELETS, NECKLACE WITH PENDANT).
CLOTH-COVERED DISKS WITH DYED MOOSEHAIR EMBROIDERY.
NECKLACE: 34.5 CM., WIDTH OF LARGEST DISK, 4 CM.;
BRACELETS: 19 AND 18.5 CM.; BROOCH: 5.5 X 5 CM. (20.872)

There are many cases of native people adapting to European fashion. You notice it happens more in the East than the West. When they couldn't afford to buy the latest fashions, they made their own. Adaptation encourages innovation and resourcefulness. Using only the materials you have available — sweetgrass, birchbark, moosehair, beads, and cloth — you painstakingly craft your own fashion statement, as in this Huron jewelry (fig. 84). A delicate and exquisite piece of work, it could also be regarded as tourist art. Whatever the reason for its creation, however, it is a special piece that was meant to be worn. Just imagine the bracelet and necklace contrasted against a white blouse — it would look absolutely spectacular. The floral motifs are all crafted in natural moosehair and show influences of European embroidery and traditional tufting techniques.

IDEALS AND STEREOTYPES

I think it's important to demystify some of our ideas about who we are. So often we are thought of as the stoic Indian riding on the plain or riding off into the sunset. That is such a romantic, stereotypical image, the kind that people love — these images help people evade dealing with some of the other social issues of native identity. We often encourage that image of "the Indian" ourselves. For instance, if I go on parade I'll put on my leather fringe jacket, my war bonnet, and stand by a tipi. I'll do all the things you want me to do in order to convince you I'm an Indian. We have sometimes perpetuated stereotypes of Indians, and that has to change. And changing means looking at ourselves and recognizing that we're like everybody else in this world — we have good guys, we have bad guys. We have a spiritual mantle as well as a sense of humor. Maybe because we

tend to idealize it, I think we sometimes look at our cultural past too seriously.

We native peoples have idealized ourselves. We tend to think that our world view is pristine, untouched, uninfluenced by European culture. And that's not true. In any kind of living culture, that culture is constantly changing and evolving.

What we also have to consider is that outside the community, popular culture — movies and books, for example — has really isolated us culturally. Everybody has idealized us as well. So native people begin to think that in order to be legitimately Iroquoian, for example, they have to act in a certain way and they have to be approached accordingly.

In many ways, the objects provide something of an antidote to the stereotypes. Coming from a background in art history, I look at works from an aesthetic point of view. But I also regard the works from a Konadahah Seneca perspective — in terms of what the pieces mean to me, culturally and emotionally. In working through the museum's collections, I have also become aware of the technical virtuosity of the pieces and of the ways in which they relate to the passage of life — to youth, the middle years, and old age.

I was thinking of myself growing up, seeing my grandmother making dolls, seeing my grandfather make little toys, seeing my aunts and uncles and neighbors make toys for us to play with. And I'd like to see a case in the museum that's scaled for children, so that we adults have to get down on our knees to look and see what is going on. In this case we could put those wonderful miniatures, the dolls, and other objects — some done for tourists but some done just for the sheer fun of it — that are almost like toys, that have a sense of humor.

TOURIST ART

I have a definite interest in tourist art. Whether we like it or not, tourists now have impacted our culture. And we've got to come to terms with it. I'm going to do a show on bingo! On the reserve you have new bingo fetishes. You sit there at a table and you see all these Indian women with their little good-luck charms and beaded cigarette cases — you can see these things in a blue haze in these bingo parlors. All of this is very much part of what is taking place in the culture.

When we talk about tourist art, granted, the old adage "popularity breeds mediocrity" sometimes applies. In the early days of the tourist trade, techniques certainly changed, as the *raison d'être* for the objects changed. People began making objects not necessarily for their own use, but for the white tourist who wanted to take something back from his experience visiting a Native American community. (Of course, this type of

FIGURE 85
HURON PINCUSHION.
MOOSEHAIR EMBROIDERY AND BEADS, 19 X 73 CM. (22.4677)

exchange has been going on since Contact — in fact, I would love to see the kind of tourist art taken back to Europe long ago.) If you think about argillite carving from the Haida of the Queen Charlotte Islands, you will note that it developed during the early nineteenth century because the European demand for these unusual carvings was as insatiable as the Haida's need for trade goods. Argillite is heavy and fragile and had no practical application within the Haida community, except for its use in those carvings that prompted the extraordinary interest of European buyers. Haida aesthetics and innovation were supremely important to these Haida artisans; thus, by the twentieth century, what began primarily as tourist art was now accepted as part of the legitimate, more expensive art market.

The late nineteenth and early twentieth centuries also saw the proliferation of curios from eastern tribes that were developed solely for the souvenir market. Sometimes called whimsies, these souvenirs reflected the ornate tastes preferred by Victorians; unlike the Haida argillite carvings, whimsies had no particular tradition that identified them as Indian, except for the technique of beading — a European tradition that in the minds of many tourists was now associated with Indian culture. Constructed from European materials, these items served as pincushions, picture frames, match and whisk holders, and ladies' purses; their primary purpose, however, was to serve as souvenirs.

Whimsies took on multi-shaped forms — high-button shoes, flowers, ladies' hats, parasols, and birds, for example — and were elaborately beaded in true souvenir fashion to announce the place and date of purchase. Beads were used in great proliferation — this beaded pincushion, for example, fea-

FIGURE 86
IROQUOIS BROOCH WITH MASONIC EMBLEM DESIGN.
SILVER, 3.2 X 5 CM. (24.4617)

tures so much decoration, there's no room to put pins in it (fig. 85). This item, however, is an excellent transitional piece and reflects traditional moosehair tufting or bristle technique alongside raised beadwork.

SELECTIONS
This silver brooch belonged to Captain Joseph Brant (Mohawk, 1742–1807), an Iroquois war chief (fig. 86). As the Iroquois began to adapt, many, particularly the Christian Mohawks, joined organizations like the Free Masons. What I find fascinating about these pieces of silver is that the artists have taken something that's already established and have manipulated it. So those very early Masonic silver pins and brooches are all of a sudden adapted and now those images become part of our cultural milieu.

✖

Texture, line, contrast, space — they are all considered in this piece, a Delaware deerskin bag (fig. 87). These are the four basic elements that contemporary artists have to deal with and that these people had to deal with. Their methods were intuitive — they had an inherent understanding of the aesthetic principles at work, and they took off from there. I suspect that a strong spiritual sense motivated them. They believed that human beings were to maintain a balance between physical and spiritual needs — this world view often manifested itself in articles such as smoke bags. Symmetry in design was a way to recognize the balance between the two forces. So these smoke bags, used to carry tobacco and pipes, had very powerful images.

✖

I remember my grandmother making me a *gustoweh* (headdress) — a cloth one, it wasn't traditional — and saying, "You have to have one" (fig. 88). I didn't quite understand what she was saying. Coming much later than the traditional fashion, it was made in a very European way — a raised skullcap with beadwork on it and a tufting of feathers on the top. What she really was saying was that the ideas that are incorporated in this hat, or in this design and the use of the materials, have to go on. You have to understand that.

ELDERS

In Iroquoian thinking, at least at Grand River, we believe that life can be metaphorically compared to a circle. You begin life as a child, and pass around the circle making your contribution to society, only to arrive as an elder at the point on the circle where you began as a child. It is here where your children must now care for you as you begin your spiritual journey to the land of the Creator. As an elder, the spiritual elements become foremost in your mind and the images or the designs you make often draw upon the interconnections between the physical and spiritual worlds. In more traditional households, children and elders have special relationships, as elders become very actively involved in the child's spiritual welfare. Our culture is not static but dynamic and ongoing, and we were placed on Turtle Island to re-create the good works of creation.

In spite of the demands of the highly technological society in which we now live, our culture is still flourishing as it was meant to, in the legacy of our ancestors.

· 194 ·

FIGURE 87
LENAPE BAG.
DEERSKIN WITH QUILLS, TIN CONES, AND FEATHERS,
28.5 X 21.3 CM. (13.5886)

FIGURE 88
SENECA *GUSTOWEH* (HEADDRESS).
LEATHER WITH SILVER BAND, WAMPUM BEADS, AND FEATHERS,
50.7 X 61 CM. (6.354)

A Pomo basket-weaver from northern California, **Susan Billy** learned the art from her great-aunt Elsie Allen, whom she sees as a woman "standing in the doorway of changing times." For Susan Billy and her great-aunt, as for other Pomo basket-weavers, issues of assimilation, adaptation, and acculturation are of central importance. Billy, who is also an accomplished jewelry-maker and owner of a bead store in Ukiah, California, regards her people's baskets as a primal connection to the past. She is especially interested in the techniques and styles used by other weavers.

The baskets, which Billy sees as living things, are dynamic examples of traditional Pomo values. The baskets reveal "the attention to detail and the great respect our weavers and people have toward nature."

"Sometimes I get sad because today we do not have very many old weavers left — there are only a handful of women and a few men making baskets. But I get very upset when I hear people say that weaving is a dying art and that nobody is doing it, because I'm here, I'm doing it. And I know that there are others also weaving. I feel that there is always somebody who is going to carry on that wisdom and that knowledge."

SUSAN BILLY

My Great-Aunt Elsie Allen

When I was growing up I had a great respect for the baskets. I was brought up on the east coast of Virginia, so I was not raised among my people or around these traditions, but we had several baskets in our home and I was always drawn to them and fascinated by them. The baskets were revered in our family. From the time I was very young, I would ask my father how this or that basket started, how it ended, and what materials it was made from. I had a lot of questions, but he was not able to answer them for me. Still I would continue to ask my father and he would give me the same reply: "Some day you can look up Elsie Allen." And so I carried that name around in my heart and it resonated within me. I did not meet her until many years later when I showed up on her doorstep.

I was living in Berkeley at the time. One morning it just seemed like the right time to leave, so I moved to Mendocino County that day. I moved into my grandmother's house, which my grandfather had built at the turn of the century and in which no one had lived since my grandmother had passed away. I knew that Elsie lived in the next town. Come February of 1974, after I got settled in a bit, I knocked on Elsie's door and when she answered it I said, "You don't know me. My name is Susan Billy and I am your relative. All my life my father told me I could look you up and that you would help me and tell me the answers to my questions. I am here to learn about the Pomo baskets."

She was amazed that in these late times there was anyone who wanted to learn about the baskets. She had always hoped that some of the younger Indian people would want to learn this art, but they became so busy in their lives — with cars and televisions, and all these modern things — that they weren't really interested in the baskets any more.

"You know, I started a class yesterday and nobody showed up," Elsie said. "I'm teaching on Tuesdays and Thursdays, so if you come tomorrow it will be the first class and you will not have missed anything." I said that sounded good. When I showed up the next morning, she handed me an awl and knife and said, "These are the only tools you will need as a basket-weaver. They belonged to your grandmother and I realized last night that I was just taking care of them for you." It was a very emotional experience, quite overwhelming. I had these tools and I could just feel that I was where I was supposed to be. And I began to sit with her and learn from her for the next sixteen years.

Elsie made many feathered baskets and the *dau* in these baskets sometimes consisted of a feather in a different color.

SUSAN BILLY WITH ELSIE ALLEN, CA. 1980.

PHOTO: *UKIAH DAILY JOURNAL*.

POMO WOMAN WITH BASKET.

PHOTO BY GRACE NICOLSON. (P19036)

· 199 ·

FIGURE 89
POMO THREE-STICK COILED BASKET.
SEDGE ROOT, WILLOW; MEADOWLARK, MALLARD,
AND QUAIL TOPKNOT FEATHERS; AND CLAM AND ABALONE SHELL,
3.7 X 20.2 CM. DIAM. (23.6864)

THE DAU

The *dau* is what we call the spirit door. It is an intentional irregularity in the design. For some weavers, there is always a dau in a Pomo basket (fig. 90). It is a place where any kind of sadness, any feeling that you wouldn't want in the basket, has a way to be free, to get out. It is also there to allow all good spirits to come in and freely circulate in the basket. The dau is absolutely at the weaver's discretion — she decides how to incorporate it into the basket. Sometimes it takes the form of a very obvious variation in the pattern. Sometimes it's just a tiny break of one stitch in the design; or it might just be one or two little stitches making an opening. Some believe that if there is a solid pattern or a band in the basket, it always needs a dau so the spirit can move freely. Quite

FIGURE 90
BAMTUSH-WEAVE BASKET, CA. 1900–1930.
MADE BY MARY BENSON (1876–1930), POMO. REDBUD AND WILLOW,
10.1 X 18.2 CM. DIAM. THE *DAU* CAN BE SEEN IN THE TWO
UNCONNECTED TRIANGLES. (24.2139)

often — especially with baskets that have isolated designs that aren't connected — it can be difficult to find the dau. Many weavers put them in, while some never do. It is very deliberate — even for one weaver it will not always be the same from basket to basket. Sometimes the dau is very subtle and sometimes very obvious. Oftentimes there will be many bands on the basket and the daus will line up on each band; sometimes they will be completely opposite. There's no rule at all when it comes to the dau — not even one that says there must always be one.

In looking at the museum's collections, I came across pieces in which it was difficult, if not impossible, to find the dau. I gave up the search with some of them because the time was so short.

BEAUTIFUL SYMMETRY

The dau is one of the elements that really fascinates me about the baskets here, and about Pomo baskets in general. The first thing I look at is the overall basket, and the feeling that I get from it. Then I look at how it starts — the very beginning of the basket — and how it's finished, and how the pattern changes. One of the things that really intrigues me is the attention to detail. I look at the inside of the basket, I look at the outside, the shape, the color arrangement, the contrast, the light and dark areas. The endless variety of patterns really amazes me.

Several elements are important to me when I look at a basket. First, the overall finished basket itself and the attention to detail it reveals. For example, the design of this particular basket is simple and yet very striking (fig. 91). When I hold this basket, it feels almost overwhelming and vibrant to me. Its legacy, which has been passed down for so many generations, is evident when you see a basket like this. A basket like this is just as beautiful on the inside as it is on the outside. Second, the function: this basket, used for the ritual washing of a newborn baby or for a young girl when she becomes a woman, indicates the great respect for ceremonies that have been handed down from generation to generation. And third, ornamentation; for example, the clamshell beads and quail topknots that appear at the top signify the ceremonial use of this basket. Generally, the male quail topknots are used on the standard-size baskets, but in later years when smaller baskets were being made, the female quail topknots

were used because they were smaller, though they do not have as nice a curve as the male feathers.

That's what I consider when I look at these baskets of our finest weavers — the keen attention to detail, the symmetry and arrangement of feathers and beads, and the colors and patterns of the baskets that they made. There have been thousands and thousands of Pomo baskets made; many of them are not only utilitarian, but are absolutely beautiful as well.

SOME TECHNIQUES

All our containers were baskets — all of our vessels for cooking, storage, gathering. We ate out of baskets. The many techniques of weaving created an incredible assortment of styles for each different kind of use.

Among our people, both men and women were basketmakers. Everything in our lifestyle was connected to those baskets. Our lives were bound the way the baskets were bound together. Generally, our women made the coiled, twined, and feathered baskets, while men made all the fishing weirs, bird traps, and baby baskets.

We use four main materials today to make baskets: sedge root, willow, redbud, and bulrush root (commonly called black root). More recently, rattan was occasionally used because of its uniformity and accessibility. Miniature foundations were usually made of bulrush root because the material was more supple than willow.

FIGURE 91
POMO THREE-STICK COILED BASKET.
SEDGE ROOT, BULRUSH ROOT, WILLOW, WITH SHELL BEADS AND QUAIL TOPKNOT FEATHERS,
13.5 X 30 CM. DIAM. (4.8786)

Some people have their own unique style. William Benson, one of the few truly accomplished male Pomo basket-weavers, used *po*, or "Indian gold," as a base for some of his baskets. Po is magnesite, a white stone that turns a gold color when fired. Benson used it unfired. The use of Indian gold in his baskets was very unusual (fig. 92). He is the only one I know of to use po in his baskets, although I have learned that a few others did too.

There are a variety of weaving techniques used in making Pomo baskets. Among the most well known and recognized are one-willow coiled work and the three-willow foundation. We weave several styles of twined baskets, such as two-strand twining, three-strand twining (fig. 93), and lattice twining. Wicker weave was utilized for work baskets. Initially, the Pomo traded their baskets for bags of flour and sugar. Miniature baskets became popular for

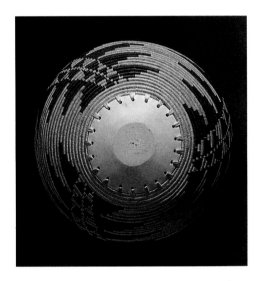

FIGURE 92
THREE-STICK COILED BASKET, CA. 1900–1930
MADE BY WILLIAM BENSON (1862–1930), POMO.
SEDGE ROOT, BULRUSH ROOT, WILLOW, WITH MAGNESITE DISK,
7.6 X 12.7 CM. DIAM. (24.2136)

trading because they used less materials and took less time to make. Gradually, a considerable collectors' market arose. Miniatures are the only Pomo baskets that were made specifically for trading purposes.

A SENSE OF PERFECT BALANCE

The baskets feel very much alive to me — it's this all-pervasive feeling that I get. When I look at the Pomo baskets and hold them, I feel a real connection to the past, to all the grandmothers who have gone before me. And I get a sense of calm, a sense of perfect balance. Ultimately, only the weaver knows what is going on with a particular basket; we can speculate, but it's hard to say — it takes so long to make a basket, every stitch is deliberate.

A lot of times, the baskets are so perfect that I am convinced the weaver was very centered when she made it, and I find it revealing to study these baskets. Sometimes I get sad

FIGURE 93

THREE-STRAND TWINED BASKET. MADE BY MARY BENSON (1876–1930), POMO.

REDBUD AND WILLOW, 13.9 X 18.1 CM. DIAM. (24.2125)

because today we do not have very many old weavers left — there are only a handful of women and a few men making baskets. But I get very upset when I hear people say that weaving is a dying art and that nobody is doing it, because I'm here, I'm doing it. And I know that there are others also weaving. I feel that there is always somebody who is going to carry on that wisdom and that knowledge. Which reminds me that a lot of our songs have been lost. But they're only lost for now, they are not really gone. Elsie Allen used to tell me that the lost songs would come through at some time in the future, they will come through to young people in their dreams. The songs aren't gone — they may be in the rocks now, or somewhere down by the river, or someplace. She felt very strongly that they are just waiting for the right person to bring them out again.

Weaving is very repetitious, but the true difficulty lies in the discipline required — having the desire and discipline to take the time to prepare the materials. If I don't feel good inside, I cannot sit down with my basket. I don't go to the basket for comfort or therapy. I have to feel good in order to weave. If I feel bad when I start to weave, these bad feelings will be reflected in my work — I would find myself breaking willows, and so forth.

When I finish a basket, I feel really complete. I put a part of me into the piece that I have worked on. We have a tradition that when we finish a basket we turn it over and put the awl, the knife, and the last little piece that we cut off on top of it. Traditionally, we let that sit for four days so that the basket comes to completion. So even though you finish it right then and take the last stitch, it's still not done. I usually feel really good about finishing a basket because I've brought something from beginning to end. Sometimes, though, I know I get very attached to my baskets. Sometimes I feel sad because I know that it is going to go away from me. I grow really close to the baskets and I feel like I am going to miss that basket — yet I know it is going to

be out there somewhere.

As I said, these baskets are still alive. They all have an energy to them. I may not know the basket-maker's intention or the thoughts behind a particular basket, but I know something special is in every single one. It couldn't have been made without this quality. This ties in with ceremonial baskets that are put out with no physical thing being placed inside them. The basket itself carries exactly what needs to be present at the ceremony. When the women made those ceremonial baskets for someone highly regarded — a medicine person or chief — and they were working on a piece that was going to be used for doctoring, they had to be very careful about what their thoughts were.

CEREMONIAL BASKETS

People frequently ask me what these ceremonial baskets held. They did not have to hold anything because the basket itself was all that was needed. The basket contained the prayers and the wonderful, good energy that made it a ceremonial basket. The women were very strict when they were making baskets for the medicine people or for a specific purpose. The women would fast for several days before working on the basket. Elsie Allen would sometimes have a dream that she was supposed to make a basket for a particular person, and then would wake up very early the next morning and work until she became weak with hunger and fatigue. Only then would she put the basket down and get something to eat. She would not work on the basket again until the next day, after she had fasted through the night.

Pomo baskets can take months and even years to finish. One of the most powerful things about these baskets is the great respect that was paid to ancestors, materials, and spirits. Among the elders with whom I was close, what was most striking was the respect that they had for everything, for all living things.

When a child was born it would be put into a baby carrier. Traditionally, a basket was not made before a child was born and the men made the baby baskets. The uncle would make the basket, so when a woman would go into labor and give birth to her child, the uncle would be called in. The materials would already be prepared, because they would have to be dried. There would be some preparation, but the basket itself was not yet made. The uncle would show up the day the child was born and work on that basket and nothing else for three days. Food would be brought to him, everything was brought to him, and for three days he did nothing but work on that basket. On the third day he would come back to his niece's house in the evening when he was done. You can make a baby carrier in three days if you don't have to do anything else.

TIME

Basketmaking is very time-consuming; it is not a quick process, something that gives you an immediate result. We have to gather our materials at just the right time and in the right season and cure them for one year before we use them. The actual weaving is really at the end of the process. It could take months or years to make a basket. It's a very long journey, calling for much patience.

Many of the baskets that I have seen at the museum took many years to finish. I remember saying to my good friend Laura Somersal, who was in her late eighties then (she was almost a hundred when she passed away), "Laura, this basket is taking me forever. I have been working on it for a year and a half." And she said, "Oh, honey, don't worry about it," and she picked up a basket and said, "I started this basket thirty-three years ago and it's still about, oh, maybe halfway, two-thirds done." She made me feel that I didn't have to pressure myself. She reaffirmed my belief that my time, and how I handle my time and my work,

is just how it is supposed to be, because sometimes it takes me a long time.

POMO

The word "Pomo," which some believe is derived from Poma, the name of a particular village, was given to us by anthropologists at the turn of the century. Because of the similarities of our basketry and cultures, anthropologists conveniently saw us as one group. Actually, there are more than seventy different tribes, within what is known as Pomo country. We originally had seven different languages, but today there are only three that are still spoken. In terms of basketry, however, there is a commonality in our weaving — in the longstanding tradition of shapes, materials, and techniques we use.

TABOOS

Women are not supposed to weave baskets when they are menstruating. This is one of our taboos. Bleeding is considered a powerful time — a time of power and intuition. The women chose to remove themselves during their "kela" by isolating themselves in "moon huts." Husbands were not allowed to fish or hunt while their wives were menstruating, and the women were not allowed to prepare food. By adding to her basket one to four stitches of quills from a medicine bird called the flicker, however, the menstruating weaver could continue to work.

Once I went to a beadmaking class even though I was menstruating, and the teacher eventually left the room and moved into the hallway. When I described to Elsie Allen what had happened, she replied that somehow the teacher knew that I had my period and that she could not be around it. The teacher was a medicine woman and she had to leave the room in order to protect herself, because when they do their medicine they have to do things just right. There's still a lot I don't know. There's still a lot to learn.

Member of the executive committee of the Delaware tribe for twelve years (and vice president for three), **Linda Poolaw** is also a health researcher, playwright, curator, and educator. She taught a photo-documentation class at Stanford University and curated a Kiowa photography exhibition that involved collaboration with the Kiowa people. She presently works for the University of Oklahoma Health Sciences Center at the Anadarko Indian Health Clinic in Anadarko, Oklahoma, investigating the causes of heart disease among Indians.

Half Kiowa and half Delaware, Poolaw feels her background gives her insight into both cultures. She wants to help her people preserve, study, and wonder about their cultural traditions — to foster pride among young people and, through knowledge, enhance their sense of identity.

"When we were growing up, we were taught that you don't ask questions. You just have to stay around and listen and the answer will come to you. Just keep thinking about it, and you'll get your answer."

LINDA POOLAW

· 209 ·

Personal History

My father is Kiowa and my mother Delaware, and although I've been brought up as a Delaware person, I have deep respect for all cultures. I enrolled as a Delaware because the Delaware people are matriarchal and it was easier to follow my mother. Being part of both cultures has been good for me — you don't have this tunnel vision suggesting one way is the only way. I had to respect all.

The Kiowa and Delaware are vastly different tribes. The Kiowa are a nomadic, Plains culture, while the Delaware are a Woodlands culture. There was a lot of teasing at home as a result of having parents from two native cultures, and with two brothers who are enrolled Kiowa. For example, the Kiowas once ate turtles, while my Delaware mother's family belongs to the Turtle Clan. It was unique growing up in that situation — my father's family ate turtles and my mother's family did not and there was always a lot of teasing about it. That's how I was taught to deal with the hardships of life — through laughter, humor, teasing. That's how you get along and survive.

I've written three plays, including a children's play.

One play, which I wrote at the University of Oklahoma, is called *Happiness is Being Married to a White Woman.* It's very contemporary — I was taking shots at people, especially at Indian men who go out and marry white women and bring them back to the community and expect everybody to accept the woman. In the play, it's hard for the woman and for the Indian. She's a very aggressive woman who makes lots of mistakes, thinking that she could run the whole household white-woman fashion — a household that includes the grandpa, who by culture couldn't even talk to her, and this kind of thing. It ends up okay, and everyone has a lot of fun.

The Community

I participated in this project because I want to bring a lot of hope back to the community. When you're dealing with Indian people and the sensitive nature of a lot of these artifacts, there's always some controversy over what can be shown and what shouldn't be shown. But I've been told by my elders — go up there and find out what's there, we want to know what's there. They're curious too about what's in the museum's collection. I see the whole process as a learning experience.

I've witnessed the breakdown of our Indian culture and communities, and the lack of identity. In most Indian-populated areas, there is nothing to motivate people to research their heritage. I am hopeful that we will get enough young Indian people interested in preserving, studying, and wondering about their past. It may take time, but I think there are many young people out there who are willing to do it. I just hope that it's not too late, that enough of our young people become interested before the past is all gone.

There are some very positive signs of community interest in native cultures. When I taught a class in photo-documentation at Stanford University, I took my students back home to Oklahoma, to the Kiowa community to do research on my father's photographs. Most of the photographs weren't labeled and we didn't know who the people in the pictures were. All we knew was that most of the pictures were taken around sixty years ago.

I was concerned about bringing these young people home with me — most of them had had very little contact with Indians and I wasn't sure if this would work. But I was really more frightened of the Indian people than of anything else. I was afraid they would say, "Get out of here, we don't want to talk to you." But at some point, after turning on the tape recorders and looking at

DELAWARE WOMAN WEARING A COMPLETE TRADITIONAL OUTFIT,
INCLUDING RIBBONWORK BLANKET. NEAR BARTLESVILLE, OKLAHOMA.
PHOTO BY M.R. HARRINGTON. (N3159)

GEORGE POOLAW (KIOWA),
THE FATHER OF THE PHOTOGRAPHER, HORACE POOLAW.
JOHN O'LEARY COLLECTION.
NATIONAL ANTHROPOLOGICAL ARCHIVES,
SMITHSONIAN INSTITUTION.

(LEFT TO RIGHT) HANNAH KEAHBONE, ANNA POOLAW SAUNKEAH,
SINDY KEAHBONE, MARTHA KOOMSA, AND UNIDENTIFIED WOMAN.
OKLAHOMA CITY, OKLAHOMA, CA. 1930.
PHOTO BY HORACE POOLAW.
HORACE POOLAW PHOTOGRAPHY PROJECT, STANFORD UNIVERSITY.

two thousand photographs, the people were just wonderful. The Kiowas really wanted to talk because they were seeing images in those photographs that some of them could just remember and that their grandchildren had never seen. They were dragging their grandchildren in, saying "Look at my grandma, look at my grandpa." I know it brought back memories.

Impatient Society

If we're looking for truth about our people, it's not in the textbooks and it's not anywhere where we can pop it up on a computer, the way the white man's education wants us to do — the white system wants us to hurry up and find something and read it and go take a test and pass it and, suddenly, you know it and you're smart. When we were growing up, we were taught that you don't ask questions. You just have to stay around and listen and the answer will come to you. Just keep thinking about it, and you'll get your answer. And we weren't told a lot of things because at that time it was felt we couldn't understand it — couldn't understand the answers. Eventually, all the answers you need come to you.

FIGURE 94
KIOWA PEYOTE FAN.
OKLAHOMA. DEERSKIN, BEADS, BRAIDED
CORDING, AND EAGLE FEATHERS,
LENGTH 75.5 CM. (5.65)

We are now living in an impatient society that doesn't allow for this process — we have to go to the library or call information so we can have our answers immediately. We're always in a hurry.

But I see with the museum's collection that we can visit it again and again, and yet there will always be something that is going to be missed. There will be something that somebody else is going to find that we have not noticed. Everyone comes with a different frame of reference. It's all here, we just have to take the time to find it. That will be the beauty and balance of the learning process.

I had trouble, for example, identifying, or speaking very insightfully about, the male dress, male weapons, and other male artifacts because I don't know about them. I can look at them and recognize materials, but I don't know about them because I am not supposed to know about them. And there are some things that I couldn't talk about — for example, some religious objects. I won't touch any peyote material, such as the loose fan (fig. 94). I don't know how something like this was used inside the peyote tipi because I was never allowed to enter it. When I was growing up, only men were allowed in the peyote tipi. I understand that women are now allowed in to some meetings. So, to fully identify everything would be almost impossible — you'd need a male and a female tribal member for identification. Women know things that men don't and vice versa.

MY GREAT-GRANDMOTHER

I have started work on a book about my great-grandmother Kaw-Au-In-On-Tay (Goose that Honks), a Mexican who was captured by the Kiowas. It was difficult getting information about her from my father. He related bits and pieces about her capture, but little else. He was very proud of her. I did gain some knowledge, however, from his older sister Margaret, who died recently. She was the last of her generation. She told me some valuable information about my great-grandmother, who was a pretty amazing woman. She died in 1927, but we have photographs of her.

She was captured in Sonora, Mexico, by a raiding band of Kiowas when she was twelve years old. She grew up a Kiowa woman. She danced the Ghost Dance. I still have her Ghost Dance dress.

GHOST DANCE

The Ghost Dance of the Kiowa started around the time that the Sun Dance was outlawed in 1890. Around 1923, the last Ghost Dance was held. There are no ornaments — beads, for example — attached to Ghost Dance dresses. They are very simple. The colors are just the blue, the green, and the yellow (fig. 95). The Ghost Dance dress that I own has the same colors. The women who could wear Ghost Dance dresses — and not everyone could

— were special people who participated in the Ghost Dance ceremony. My father's other sister, Anna Saunkeah, told me about the Ghost Dance of Wovoka: a new belief originating in the West, probably Nevada, that came upon the Kiowa people. It was soon outlawed under heavy pressure from the missionaries and the United States government.

The Ghost Dance is remembered as the last tie with the Indian world before the Christian world took over; it is very important that we show that the Ghost Dance did happen and that Plains Indians were fighting for their own religion.

I think it can be shown that we did have a religion — the Ghost Dance. And many Kiowas participated in it.

KIOWA AND DELAWARE TRADITIONS

By the turn of the century, beads were beginning to be more accessible, so you start seeing more and more beads on Kiowa garments and cradleboards. Babies and younger people were highly honored — families did without so that children could have things that looked nice. That's why you see a lot of beautifully decorated baby clothes and toys. So much work was put into those things because the children were very special.

It should be remembered that the Kiowa people, like the Comanche and other Plains groups, didn't have a lot of time to sit around and create this remarkable material. They were moving all the time — hunting, gathering, and tanning hides (and if you've ever tanned a hide, you know how long it takes). It's easy to look at all these things and just see the surface; really understanding what goes into the actual construction is another matter. With some of the baby carriers, for example, you have to

FIGURE 95
KIOWA GHOST DANCE DRESS.
OKLAHOMA. DEERSKIN, LENGTH 147.5 CM. (2.1673)

start with a cedar backboard, then you tan the hides, then you have to find the right beads. And bear in mind that when it comes to this kind of beadwork, you don't just pick up a bunch of beads and start in. When beads come to you, they are in different sizes, and in order to have a really good-looking piece of beadwork, you've got to get all the sizes exactly right. That's what makes your design. If you use a big bead and then a little one, your design is not going to look very good or very neat.

✖

Kiowa beadwork designs reflect the people's nomadic lifestyle. Their designs are geometrical and sometimes based on dreams and visions. They use a lot of white in the backgrounds, probably to bring out the designs (fig. 96). You can see Christian influence in the design of this pouch because there is a tipi or church with crosses.

✖

Delaware designs, on the other hand, reflect a more sedentary Woodlands lifestyle in which people had time to sit

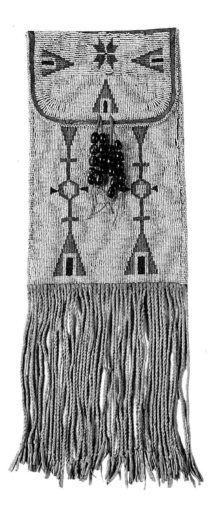

FIGURE 96
KIOWA BEADED BAG.
OKLAHOMA. HIDE; BEADED, BRAIDED CORDING;
TIN CONES, 52 X 19 CM. (12.868)

and observe nature, and thereby copy or imitate it more realistically (fig. 97). I understand that the lacework pattern on this pouch was actually copied from French lace that the Delaware saw in Canada.

The women who made these objects were very vain people. They cared what other people thought about them. They would make this cradleboard for other people to see. This kind of work raises your station, enhances your reputation, within the tribe. I was teased one time when I began beadworking — people said, "you're trying to be like Aho." Aho was probably one of the best Kiowa bead-workers of her time. Everything she did, including the way she kept house, was very neat. I am told that the time you put into your work is reflected onto your life. Vanessa Morgan, a Kiowa bead-worker, told me that how you look reflects on your husband and raises his station within the tribe. Recently, I wrote about this in a photography catalogue and was criticized by non-Indian women who said, "that's not very feminist." I'm sorry for their not understanding, but that's the way it was and that's the way the society worked.

✖

FIGURE 97

MUNSEE DELAWARE POUCH, CA. 1870.

ONTARIO, CANADA. CLOTH, BEADS, AND RIBBON, 17 X 14.5 CM. (24.1461)

Eagle-feather headdresses were worn by men of stature in the tribe, such as a war chief or spiritual chief (fig. 98). Not everyone could wear one. My grandfather, Kiowa George, owned one and wore it with pride. He was the Sweathouse Doctor of the tribe, the Calendar Keeper, and a renowned arrow-maker. He attained these positions of prominence by being a good warrior and leader.

THE KIOWAS AND DELAWARES

Kiowa history has its roots around where the Yellowstone River in the north comes to a fork. The Kiowa probably came from Canada in earlier times — some of the artifacts that they brought down with them and some of the words that they still had in their language suggest this. "White bear," for example, occurs in the names of people in the tribe and is probably a reference to the polar bear. In any case, they eventually ended up on the Southern Plains, at the

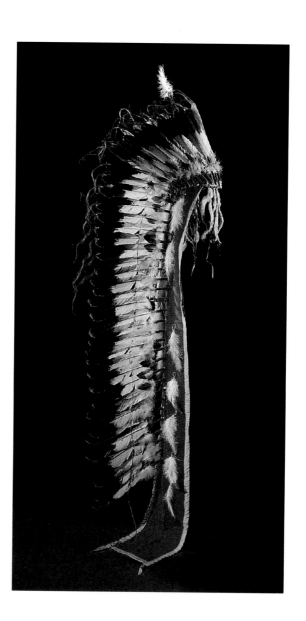

FIGURE 98
KIOWA HEADDRESS.
CLOTH, EAGLE FEATHERS, ERMINE, HORSEHAIR, AND BEADS,
LENGTH 190 CM. (2.8375)

west end of the Wichita Mountain Range in southwestern Oklahoma, where history really finds them in the early 1800s. They attempted their last Sun Dance in 1890, when they were run off by the U.S. soldiers from Fort Sill. By the time of Oklahoma statehood in 1907, the Kiowas were living on their allotments in frame homes. At that point, we were well into transition to the present.

The Delaware people were from here — the New York, New Jersey, and Pennsylvania area. We started moving earlier than anybody, I think. We were pushed out into Pennsylvania, Ohio, Indiana, Missouri. My group, the Absentee Delaware, separated around what is now Missouri — south of St. Louis, a place called Cape Girardeau. The main group went into what is now Kansas, and my group went into Arkansas, then Texas. We were mostly with Wichitas and Caddos (the Caddos had been moved into the Brazos Valley by that time) and also with the small remnant of Cherokees. We were there probably around twenty, twenty-five years, maybe a little bit longer. The Delawares and all of their movement had a history of affiliation with the white man — some of us knew how to speak English and so we were used as scouts. We worked as scouts with Sam Houston and were famous for this. Then we were moved again into southwestern Oklahoma in the mid 1800s.

When he was in Texas, my great-grandfather Jack Harry — along with, I think, a Shawnee man and a Pawnee man (I'm not really sure about the Pawnee, but there was a Shawnee man) — used to make little visits to old Mexico, where he was actually given a land grant. At this time we had all been moved en masse into Caddo County, southwestern Oklahoma. But he was still looking for that Utopia somewhere, so he kept going back into old Mexico. I understand that the trees and mountains in Mexico were very like where we came from here. His goal was to get us out from behind the fences. But on the way back from one of those exploratory trips, they contracted smallpox, and because he believed in sweathouses, he went into the sweathouse. Of course, heat and pox don't mix, and he died. But one of the men came back to tell about it. So that was it. We stayed in Caddo County and that's where we remain today.

THE DELAWARE CREATION STORY

Some tablets, discovered a hundred or so years ago, were supposed to have contained the story called the *Walam Olum* or Red Score — the Delaware creation story. As I understand it, if proven to be authentic, these tablets would have been older than the Bible. In any case, they are missing and may have been destroyed. Some Delaware historians and scholars choose not to believe in the Walam Olum because it has not been documented — there's no proof. But it's one of those things that I believe.

My mother talks of listening to stories about Nanabush, and has even heard stories about dinosaurs and that sort of thing — stories that are in the Walam Olum. There are several different copies of the Walam Olum around — my tribe has a copy of it on paper — but the actual tablets are missing. No one knows where they are. Lately there seems to be a lot of new interest in the tablets. We get inquiries all the time asking us for all kinds of explanations. But it's hard for us to respond because it's been so long since the tablets were lost and I don't know where we lost them. In any case, it's not a religion as much as a creation story.

The story talks about the ice, when the ice came and went away. The story depends to some extent on how you interpret it, but essentially it tells how the Delawares came down through the centuries. The Delawares were called the Grandfathers or the First People, and supposedly all the other people came from the Delawares, who were the oldest ones.

INDEX

PHOTOGRAPHY CREDITS

The photographers and the sources of photographic material are as follows, with copyright in the name of the photographer, unless otherwise indicated.

Photographic portraits of the following selectors are by David Neel: Begay, Billy, Conklin, Her Many Horses, Hill, McMaster, Medicine Crow, New, Nyholm, Perry, Poolaw, Ríos, and Swentzell.

Photographic portraits of the following selectors are by Karen Furth (NMAI): Fernandez and Huanca, Huatta and Cruz, Palafox and Olivares, and Puwainchir and Tsenkush, © Smithsonian Institution.

Photographic portraits of the following selectors are by Pamela Dewey (NMAI): House and Milanovich, © Smithsonian Institution.

All object photographs are by David Heald, with object preparation by mountmaker Elizabeth McKean.

All archival photographs are from the NMAI collection, unless otherwise noted in the captions.

David Neel (Kwakiutl) is a professional artist as well as photographer. Based in Vancouver, Neel works in several media — sculpture, painting, printmaking, glass, and precious metals among them. His photographs have appeared widely in magazines and on posters, and have been exhibited in museums and galleries internationally. Neel draws on his cultural heritage for his artistic direction, citing his ancestors as the "starting point" for his personal artistic interpretation.

Moccasins pictured in Fig. 46 are as follows:

6.8343	Inuit
24.1544	Navajo
2.7101	Kansa
14.3357	Wood's Cree
19.7123	Tuscarora
21.1921	Sioux
24.3662	Alaskan
19.6341	Chippewa
2.5985	Shawnee
24.4386	Cree
2.2202	Kiowa
20.5948	Arapaho
20.5868	Kiowa
22.8991	Sioux or Dakota
7.1079	Slavey
12.2127	Arapaho
18.2199	Arapaho
20.5877	Comanche
16.2326	Montagnais/Nataskwan
22.9638	Tohono O'odham
25.2635	Oneida
21.994	Nez Perce
21.3539	Chamula
20.8703	Cree
8.4686	Eastern Sioux
2.1312	Comanche
2.7386	Eastern Sioux
24.1092	Shoshone
15.4471	Algonkin
10.4450	Cheyenne
19.3690	Arapaho
16.4122	Blood